Heartbroken and Healing

Encouragement and Biblical Counsel for Wives in the Wake of Sexual Betrayal

By Mary Asher and Hannah Palmer

Foreword by Martha Peace

Heartbroken and Healing

**Encouragement and Biblical Counsel
for Wives in the
Wake of Sexual Betrayal**

By Mary Asher and Hannah Palmer

Inquire at:

Focus Publishing
Rights and Permissions
PO Box 665
Bemidji, Minnesota 56619

Cover Design by Melanie Schmidt

Scripture is taken from the New American Standard Bible
Copyright © 1960, 1962, 1963, 1968, 1971, 1972, 1973, 1975, 1977, 1995
By the Lockman Foundation. Used by permission.
ISBN: 978-1-936141-11-1

Endorsements

"The mental and emotional anguish and rage from the effects of marital betrayal are enormous and enduring. The most personal of all trust relationships is marriage, and it has been grievously violated. In counseling, I have discovered most Christian materials that attempt to address this issue are full of psychological fluff. They avoid substantial godly hope and help. Mary Asher's contribution is a refreshing exception. It is written with the care and compassion of an experienced counselor and loaded with practical biblical insight. This is the type of biblical truth that touches the soul and brings healing change."

Dr. John D. Street, Chair, MABC Graduate Program, The Master's College and Seminary

"Over the years, I have often been involved in counseling men who have been caught in the net of various kinds of sexual immorality. To help these men be restored, in the Galatians 6 :1 manner, I have found numerous books, booklets, CD and DVD materials that I have assigned to help them in the put off/put on process in this area of sanctification. Unfortunately, as I have counseled the wife who is also affected by the husband's immorality, the only material I find to provide assistance and direction for her is of a very general nature. In counseling these wives, Mary Asher came face to face with the deficiency of appropriate and specific material in this area. So she recognized the need, and with her counseling experience and training, she has developed a book that will provide specific, practical, and accurately biblical help and direction for counselors, and especially for wives. I plan to use this book, and I heartily recommend it for use by other counselors when they are called upon to help wives who have experienced the backlash of their husband's unfaithfulness."

Dr. Wayne Mack, Founder of Strengthening Ministries Training Institute, South Africa, Professor Emeritus and past Chairman of MABC at The Master's College

"When dealing with the sin of a husband's experience with pornography, church people often focus on trying to help the husband, while the innocent one (in this case the wife), is often neglected and not offered help. If she is addressed with Scripture, she is told what the Bible says rather than encouraged to explore and apply God's word on her own. In Heart Broken and Healing, Mary and Hannah do an excellent job in guiding the woman to find the comfort needed in God's word in a workbook format. In those very difficult times, women who experience the direct ramifications of their husband's sin of pornography can find direct comfort from the faithful God of all comfort through His word."

Dr. Stuart Scott, Professor in the Graduate Program at The Master's College, Fellow with the Association of Certified Biblical Counselors (ACBC)

"Marital unfaithfulness has devastating consequences. Here is a Christ-focused, biblical, hope-filled workbook for betrayed wives who are seeking to save themselves and their marriage. Common struggles with fear, anger, bitterness, hopelessness, and thoughts of suicide are clearly addressed. This is a great resource for victims of marital unfaithfulness as well as counselors seeking to help them."

Randy Patten, President of TEAM Focus Ministries, Past Executive Director of NANC, (now known as ACBC)

Dedication

This book is gratefully dedicated to the One who made it possible, "For it is God who is at work in you, both to will and to work for His good pleasure (Philippians 2:12-14). Every good fruit that is produced in my life through counseling and writing is due to the gracious provision and involvement of the Lord. It has been encouraging to look back on the Lord's work in the lives of Hannah and David. I will be eternally grateful for the work that the Lord has done in my life and in the lives of those I have grown to love. It is exciting to know that this transforming work is not unique. The Lord is also at work in the lives of many, many others. We pray that this book will be used to His glory.

Mary

I am and will always be thankful for the Lord's never-ending patience, abundant loving kindness, and faithfulness to me. David's willingness to love me when I was very unlovable for almost 18 months, his faithfulness to persevere, and his actions of love to this day are a testimony to the Lord's work in his life. I am thankful for David being my best friend through all the trials we have shared.

Soli Deo Gloria
Hannah

Acknowledgements

This book would not exist without the contributions of several people who are very special to me. My deep gratitude go to my friends Martha Zamber and Michelle Brock for proofreading the initial draft and contributing to both the literary quality and spiritual content. I am very grateful to Martha Peace for offering to contribute her Bible studies *Salvation Handbook* and *The Put-Off-Put-On Dynamic*. Much more than that, I am deeply grateful to Martha for being my mentor and friend and encouraging me in this project. First and foremost I am grateful to my husband, Marshall, who was my closest aid and motivator throughout the writing process.

There were many who prayed for us during the long writing process. May the Lord richly bless each one of you.

A special word of thanks must be given to Hannah. This book was her idea. As she struggled with the issues presented here, she searched for a book that would help her think biblically … and found nothing that was truly helpful. As a result, she proposed the book you have in your hands. The entire structure of the book is from her heart. She is very dear to me, and I hope that each of you will thank our Lord for her vision, hard work, and remarkable transparency.

It is a wonderful thing to be a child of God and His servant in this sin-plagued world. It has been thrilling to watch the Lord transform lives through the ministry of His word. Thank you Lord for bringing Hannah into my life and giving me the privilege of partnering with you and all those named above to create this workbook. Please Lord, make it useful that you may be glorified. Amen.

Mary Asher

Foreword by Martha Peace

Dear Ladies,

In all my years of counseling women, learning of a husband's pornography habit and/or infidelity is one of the most difficult and heartbreaking discoveries a wife can make. Many times, I have wept with a wife but, at the same time, given her hope that she does not have to go through this extreme trial in vain. God can and will, if she responds humbly to Him, use this for her good and His glory.

You see ladies, a wife <u>can</u> glorify God and be faithful to Him whether her husband repents or not. Of course, not all situations end as well as Hannah's. A wife may ultimately have biblical grounds for divorce, but until that is clear, there are many resources God has given to wives to protect them, and to rightly put pressure on their husbands to repent.

In *Heartbroken and Healing*, Mary Asher and Hannah Palmer have written an excellent and very clear book / Bible study that takes you from the thoughts and emotions of "finding out" all the way to "opening your heart" to God and to your husband. It guides your journey from being "devastated and crushed" to loving God more and learning to love your husband more.

If you are struggling because of your husband's sin, I highly recommend this study. It is insightful and very biblical. You will likely relate closely to Hannah as she takes you through her journey in God's amazing grace. I plan to use it for my counselees. The Scriptures <u>are</u> "alive and powerful." God will help you if you will only ask him.

> Because of His Mercies,
> Martha Peace
> Biblical Counselor and Author of *The Excellent Wife*
> and other biblical resources for hope and help.

Table of Contents

Introduction

Sexual perversion is not new. However, our modern technologies provide powerful opportunities for Satan and his henchmen to take advantage of the weakness of men and slash deeply into Christian homes, wounding marriages that might otherwise be fruitful for the Lord Jesus Christ. Pornography is pervasive in our culture and made fiendishly available at the click of a mouse. It poisons the mind and inflames the flesh, predisposing the user to even further violations of the marriage covenant: E-mail, texting and internet chat rooms allowing secret sexual conversation and eventually physical sexual betrayal. The warning from God is chilling:

Now therefore, my sons, listen to me,
and pay attention to the words of my mouth!
Do not let your heart turn aside to
[the sexually immoral woman's] ways,
Do not stray into her paths.
For many are the victims she has cast down,
and numerous are her slain.
Her house is the way to Sheol,
descending to the chambers of death.
Proverbs 7:24-27

"Her house is the way to Sheol, descending to the chambers of death". Many others are wounded in the process. Chief among them are the wives. The wounds are very deep and painful. However, our God heals. There is hope in Him. He has shown us the way to healing in His word. This workbook will guide you, day by day, in the way. May the Lord richly bless you as you trust in Him.

Mary Asher

Post Script

This book is structured around the true story of Hannah, a young woman I counseled. She and her husband were eventually reconciled and their marriage restored, but it was not immediate. This will not be the outcome in every marriage. Sin is enslaving, and your husband may not repent. However, one thing we can know with certainty: restoration pleases God. God hates divorce. Therefore, seek reconciliation. The Lord will bless you.

This book was written with restoration in view, but restoration is NOT the goal. The goal is to help you respond to your circumstances in the way that pleases the Lord. Make pleasing the Lord your goal and you will experience a lavish outpouring of God's grace regardless of the outcome.

Chapter 1
Finding Out

This is a true story. Hannah came to me for help on the first day of the most devastating experience of her life. Her experiences are real, though the names and some of the details have been changed to protect the privacy of her family. Sadly, what she went through is very common. She shares this story with you, hoping that you, too, will find comfort and healing in Christ.

Hannah's Story

Ladies, I share this to encourage you. I know the pain, the feeling of not being able to breathe or stop crying, wanting to scream and to control everything. I found hope and you can too, so keep going.

My story begins years ago, before David and I were married, when we were dating. It was only small things I noticed, such as his flirting with a waitress or friend. He once dropped me off from a date early to go meet another girl, explaining that it was someone who needed help, nothing that should concern me. I convinced myself he was fully committed to me, after all, I was head over heels in love. We became happily engaged and then married. After our wedding, I answered phone calls from girls asking for him. He took and chatted with them. I even received a letter saying it was wrong for us to have married. Each time I asked him about it, David explained it away. His reasons made sense and I would convince myself that I was overreacting. My faith in him never wavered.

Several years later, David was caught viewing pornography on the internet. In the resulting tumult, I learned that he had been exposed to pornography as a child, and he had been overtaken with this sin periodically ever since. He met with a counselor for months. Though there was no evidence of continued involvement in pornography, it took me ten months to forgive him. During this time, I struggled with thoughts of bitterness and suicide. Mainly, I became obsessed with thoughts of being trash, unworthy, unable to compete with the women in the pictures. I was overcome by hopelessness. I stopped wanting to be intimate, unable to believe he actually was emotionally and mentally with me.

Years went by. I struggled on and off with trusting him. Our relationship was filled with strife. One day, I sent him an e-mail at work. After an hour with no response, I checked his personal e-mail account to see if he was checking his e-mail. What I found changed my life. I saw an e-mail from a woman I did not know. Immediately questions went through my mind. *"Do I open it? Mark it as unread? Just trust him?"* Though I knew I was risking his anger, I opened it and read it. What I

1

saw was a series of e-mails that revealed that my husband, the man I loved, was having an affair. These e-mails were sexually explicit. Equally crushing, the e-mails revealed that I had been replaced as his friend. The messages were filled with details about our lives shared with a woman I did not know: details about the children, me, our everyday activities. I was made out to be a hard to live with wife whom he was stuck with. I was crushed, angry, and wanted to die all at once.

If you are reading this book with a broken heart, if you feel crushed, and if you're barely clinging to each day as I was, it is my prayer that my pain, my growth, the counsel I was given, the lessons I needed to learn, and the hope that only God can give will be a blessing to you. So heed the counsel, do the homework, get up the next day, and keep going! The journey to love is hard (it seems impossible), but it is not. I testify that God's blessing awaits you. Today I find joy in my marriage. Hope is there. God is faithful and will bring you through this.

I am grateful to God for bringing Mary into my life to counsel and encourage me through this journey to keep putting one foot in front of the other and keep going. She graciously kept pointing me to the Savior who knew my hurts and was the only one who could bind up my wounds.

A Word from Mary

If you recently found out about your husband's sexual sin, I know that you are hurting and most likely angry. This workbook is written to help you work through your responses in a biblical way. You may feel like your heart has been ripped right out of your body. You want to lash out, scream, have someone hold you and tell you that everything is going to be OK.

I received a call from Hannah on the day she discovered that her husband was involved in ongoing sexual sin. She needed me to be there to hold her, let her cry, and listen to how bad she was hurting. It was at Hannah's prompting that this book was created. Through her experience and the word of God, we will see that God is faithful to keep His promises to us, even when we are going through one of the deepest valleys a wife will ever experience. Throughout this workbook, you will read about Naomi's pain, anger, and despair. Then you will be guided to think biblically about these responses.

Women whose husbands have committed sexual sin experience emotional pain that is as intense as the physical pain of childbirth. In childbirth, once the baby is born the pain rapidly decreases and eventually is altogether gone. Then one day you realize that you can't even remember the pain. The immediate pain from your husband's sexual sin is constant, overwhelming, and mind-consuming. Unlike childbirth pain, it does not go away quickly. At first, it is something that you have to deal with day by day.

For most of you, when you wake up tomorrow the pain will still be there. As soon as you wake up, I want you to use this workbook to focus your attention on the Word of God and the Lord Jesus Christ. You will have daily assignments. As you faithfully do the assignment each day the Lord will use His word to heal your broken heart.

For those of you who have small children, I've made each assignment short enough to complete even during your very busy day.

A Word about "You"

This book was written to help God's children be comforted and encouraged while suffering the consequences of marital betrayal. Throughout, whenever you read the word "you" it is presumed that you have been born again in Christ and become a child of God. If you are not sure you have been born again, or if are not sure what "born again" means, please thoughtfully read Appendix B at the back of this book.

A Word about Discretion

Hannah was immediately tempted to tell her friends about her husband's sin. But she realized that it would not be profitable for her to have her friends encouraging her to have self- pity. Hannah did not even share this with her very best friend from childhood. She was continually tempted to share her story because she wanted to be comforted by a sympathetic listener. Instead, Hannah turned to me, an older woman, for help. Her husband also sought out the help of an older godly man. It was essential for both of them to be mentored by someone they could trust. It is important for you to find an older woman who loves the Lord, is knowledgeable in God's Word, and will give you biblical counsel. (We will talk about this in detail in Chapter Two and help you choose the right woman to mentor you.)

Getting God's Perspective

Marital betrayal is devastating. God's blueprint for marriage is summed up in Genesis 2:24.

> *For this cause a man shall leave his father and his mother,*
> *and shall cleave to his wife;and they shall become one flesh.*

"One flesh." What a beautiful picture of the dreams most brides have before the wedding. It pictures an enveloping union of a man and a woman, a union that extends beyond sexual love to infiltrate all desires and goals. When that God-ordained union is damaged by infidelity, those dreams can come crashing down in an avalanche of painful emotions. At such times there is danger that hope will be swept away. For that reason, before you begin dealing with that emotional avalanche, you must anchor your hope on a rock that will not fail. That Rock is the Lord Jesus Christ.

From the end of the earth I call to Thee, when my heart is faint;
Lead me to the rock that is higher than I.
For Thou hast been a refuge for me …
He only is my rock and my salvation, my stronghold;
I shall not be greatly shaken.
Psalm 61:2-3, 62:2

Our hope is anchored in the character of God.

This I recall to my mind, therefore I have hope.
The Lord's lovingkindnesses indeed never cease,
For His compassions never fail.
They are new every morning;
Great is Thy faithfulness.
Lamentations 3:21-23

Do not fear, for I am with you;
Do not anxiously look about you, for I am your God.
I will strengthen you, surely I will help you,
Surely I will uphold you with My righteous right hand.
Isaiah 41:10

God wants you to turn to Him. Regardless of how your husband responds, God will strengthen and sustain you. The response of your husband cannot frustrate God or invalidate His promises. As you progress day-by-day through this book, you will learn of God's wonderful promises and learn the joy of trusting Him and enjoying His pleasure as you respond in loving obedience.

The Holy Spirit works through His word to provide everything we need for life and godliness. (2 Peter 1:3) So, get out your Bible and let's begin.

Day One

The betrayal you are experiencing is devastating and extremely painful. Do you feel abandoned? It is certainly natural for you to feel that way, but God is faithful. He always keeps His promises. He has promised to never leave you or forsake you. Today I want you to **know** that you are not going through this painful experience alone. Read Isaiah 43:1-3a and answer the following questions. The Lord is writing to Israel, but the truth of these verses can be comforting to believers as well.

Isaiah 43:1   How well does the Lord know you?

He created me, formed me, redeemed me, called me by my name + claimed me.

Isaiah 43:1-3a   You may feel you are drowning in grief. As you face the waters, the rivers, and the fire, what is true about God?

He will be w/ me & will not allow me to be destroyed

The waters, the rivers, and the fire represent what might cause the Israelites to be fearful. What things that you are experiencing might tempt you to be fearful?

Destruction of my marriage, destruction of self, godliness + righteousness

Verse 3a tells us why we do not have to be fearful and overwhelmed. What is that reason?

God is ours, our Holy One, our Savior who pays the ransom for us

Write verses 2 and 3a on a 3x5 card and carry it with you all day. Read the card often.

Day Two

Your grief is real. Your grief is justified. It is comparable to the death of someone dear to your heart. God knows what you are experiencing, and He loves you more than you can comprehend. Today's passage shows us how to take your grief to God.

Meditate on these verses and answer the following questions.

Psalm 55:1-2   King David was restless and distracted. Later in the Psalm he says he is in anguish, trembling, and overwhelmed. Why do you think David turned to God?

Volatility of emotions makes us distrustful of ourselves + we see that no one can solve our problems but God

Psalm 55:4-8   In these verses David expresses his feelings to God. It is helpful to pour out your heart to God. Using these verses as an example, write out a prayer expressing the feelings you are having about your circumstances.

Father I despair. Please forgive my hopelessness + my vain reaching. Father, my heart is broken & I fear that my marriage is broken beyond repair. He is not reaching out for me anymore, God. I fear it is over.

Psalm 55:12-14   David was betrayed by a very intimate companion. Write out what David had to say about his betrayer. How did David's relationship to his betrayer affect him?

His betrayer reproached him + exalted himself against David. But his betrayer was not an enemy & did not hate David. He was David's equal, his companion & acquaintance that confided & communicated & worshipped w/ David

He could not bear it. He could not hide from his betrayer

Psalm 55:16, 17, 22   Look back at the last two questions you answered. David was overwhelmed with grief, fear, and betrayal. He could have been consumed with self-pity. What did he choose to do? What does God want you to do?

He called upon the Lord, looked to Him for salvation, cried to the Lord + prayed to Him. He cast his burden on the Lord & trusted God to care for him.
Trust in God, lean on Him + communicate w/ Him

When Hannah came to me I realized the LONG road we had ahead of us. She would have loved to have me say to her, "You poor dear; just pack up and leave your husband." Biblically, I could not say this to her. I had to be very careful not to respond to her from my feminine emotions. I had to turn to the Scriptures and give her counsel from God's word and help her to think biblically each and every time we talked.

On those first few days Hannah struggled greatly with self-pity. I counseled her to replace her natural focus on her herself and the pain by focusing on actively and aggressively loving her children. I also pointed out to her that her children were watching how she was responding to David (even though they were unaware of the situation). Write down at least three things you can do today that will demonstrate love and respect for your husband with your children watching. Also write down three things that you can do to aggressively and actively love your children. (If you do not have children, choose a _woman_ in your church you can minister to.) Transfer these six things to a card you can refer to during the day. Your motivation in all of this must be to honor God. As you force yourself to do these things to God's glory, you will be lifted out of self-focus and self-pity.

Three things I can do to demonstrate love and respect for my husband in front of my children:

Three things I can do to aggressively and actively love my children:

Be affectionate w/ them individually

Get them comfy for bed

Sing them a song

Day Three

Hannah didn't want to pray, though she had been taught to pray. But never in her life did she expect to go through something like this. She had prayed for family, friends, tests, safe travel, good health, etc. But she didn't ever think she would need to pray because she experienced something devastating in her life. Those kinds of things happen to other people.

When you are hurting so deeply it is often hard to pray. You don't even know what to pray for. Because you are hurting so bad, you may not even have any thoughts about God.

In Romans 8:26-27 God tells us that there will be times of weakness when we will not know how to pray as we should.

During those times who is there to help us? _the Spirit + our Intercessor_

The last part of verse 27 says, *"He intercedes for the saints according to the will of God."* The Apostle Paul then explains God's will for you in the rest of Chapter 8. Read verses 28-39. Write down what God is doing and will do for you.

He is working things together for my good. He knows me, calls me, justifies me, He is for me, delivered His Son for me, gives me all things + holds us close in love.

Even if you have not already prayed to God, you may have had some of the following thoughts.

- Why me, God?

- I thought I'd never experience any pain or suffering as a Christian.

- God, why did you let this happen?

- I can't go through this; this is too hard.

It is natural to have thoughts like these. But these thoughts only push you deeper into despair. Hope comes when we renew our mind through God's word. One answer to "Why me, God?" and "Why did You let this happen" is found in Romans 8:29. According to Romans 8:29, why did God let this happen?

To conform me to Jesus

After meditating on these verses, in the space below write a prayer to God thanking Him for the work He is doing in your life. Today, each time today you have thoughts like those in the list above, read this prayer again and thank God for what He is actually doing.

Father, I know you chasten those whom you love. I know that trials test my faith & that that testing produces patience. Thank you for working in me to conform me to the image of Jesus. Thank you for Him & his example of forgiveness & love. Thank you for not separating me from your love & for working all things for my good. Thank you for accomplishing the perfect timing for your answers.

Day Four

Fix your eyes on Jesus. During these first few days, or even weeks, you will be tempted to think only about your husband's sin. Being consumed with thoughts of his sin will lead to self-pity, anger, hatred, and even revenge. Such thoughts are poison to your soul. Therefore, it is extremely important to diligently fix your eyes on Jesus Christ, who is the author and the perfecter of our faith. Read Hebrews 12:1-3 and answer the following questions.

Hebrews 12:1   We have a great cloud of witnesses surrounding us. The author of Hebrews is directing us back to chapter 11 where he reminds us of many men and women who trusted God during very difficult circumstances. Their lives testify to the faithfulness of God. Read Hebrews 11:30-40 and list all the things these men and women did because they trusted God.

B/c they trusted God, the walls of Jericho fell, Rahab received spies w/ peace, kingdoms were subdued, righteousness was worked, promises obtained, lions mouths stopped, the violence of fire quenched, sword escaped, became valiant in battle, enemies pursued, dead raised, ppl tortured w/o accepting deliverance,

Hebrews 12:1   Life is like a race. What do you need to do to be able to endure the inevitable struggles and fatigue?

Lay aside weight + sin

Today you are faced with temptations that encumber your ability to really trust God. One temptation was mentioned in today's opening paragraph. Restate that temptation below.

Continual focus on the affair keeps me from trusting God & is a weight that keeps me from running w/ endurance. It stops me in my tracks.

Write down the specific thoughts that you are having that may be interfering with fully trusting God.

I will never be enough for him. I wasn't interesting enough, skinny enough, pretty enough, alluring enough, amusing enough. I was a boring, anxious, nervous, overeating, lazy workaholic. We won't be able to fix this. We'll never escape from sexual sin

Hebrews 12:2-3   Fix your eyes on Jesus. The only way you are going to be able to put those thoughts out of your mind is to replace them with thoughts that honor God. In verses 2 and 3 what are we reminded to think about regarding Jesus?

He bookends our faith
He endured the cross, the shame & hostility of sinners
He has sat down @ the (R) hand of God

Verse 3 tells us that as we remind ourselves of the truths about Christ, we will not grow weary and lose heart. Write a prayer of thankfulness for what Jesus has done to rescue you. Re-read this prayer each time today you feel overwhelmed and betrayed.

Father,
Thank you for the humility of Jesus. Thank you for his example. Thank you for allowing us to see thru your word how Jesus ran w/ endurance. Thank you for His example that keeps me from becoming weary & discouraged.

Day Five

The pain you are enduring will seem to drain away all of your strength. You may feel like you are barely making it through the day. Some days it may take everything in you just to put one foot in front of the other to keep going. I want you to be encouraged that you do not have to walk through these days alone. God will be with you and will strengthen and comfort you.

Today we are going to meditate on Isaiah 41:10, but in order to really grasp what God is saying you need to understand what the Israelites were enduring. God's purpose in giving this prophecy is to comfort His people even in seemingly hopeless circumstances.

Isaiah 41:8-14   Read carefully looking for the kinds of threats that were frightening Israel and record them below.

Being cast away from God, ppl incensed against them, striving against them, contending w/ them, warring against them

Isaiah 41:10   Notice how God repeatedly refers to Himself. ("I am ... I am ... I will ... I will ... I will") Read Isaiah 41:10 out loud strongly emphasizing the word "I" each time it occurs. Meditate on the significance of the word "I" in this promise. Record your thoughts below.

How good is God to us? Our defender & redeemer

How do the following personal qualities of God provide strength and encouragement when we feel like we can't face the day?

God is with you. *I am not alone*

God is more powerful than anything you may have to face. *My marriage can survive & my heart can heal*

God is faithful; He always keeps His promises. *He will work things for my good*

God is personal. He cares about you and your circumstances. *He sees my value*

Isaiah 41:10   "do not anxiously look about you" If you anxiously look about you, what will you see? Is there anything or anybody out there that can keep God from taking care of you?

Only my sin will separate me from God

Isaiah 41:10   "surely ... surely" God reinforces His promise with these words. How should this affect your attitude when you feel overwhelmed? *Do we doubt God's power to perform what he has promised?*

God will uphold you. Throughout the day look for the ways that God has upheld you. Record each one below and review them tonight before you go to bed.

Good friends

Recall God's word when tempted

Your Thoughts

Chapter 2
Who Do You Tell?

Hannah's Story

Years before, when David was caught viewing pornography on the internet, I made the mistake of telling my friends. They were all sympathetic listeners, offering me a chance to tell my side of the story, cry, express my right to be upset and vent about how awful he was. Sadly, these friends, who were all believers, were unknowingly feeding my growing bitterness. I beg you not to make this mistake, not even with your best girlfriend. I learned the hard way that this is not healthy for either of you, nor for your marriage. You should seek out one or two <u>godly older</u> women to encourage you, hold you accountable, and guide you as you strive to overcome your heartache.

Even your best girlfriend may need to be left in the dark as to your deep hurt. This was the case for me. My life-long best friend, whom I will call Janet, did not know of my crushing heartache as I went through it. Though I longed to talk with her about it, I knew it was best not to. She would have come to my aid to nurse my hurt, as a good friend longs to do. She would have assured me that I had a right to grieve. But this would have fed my own feelings of bitterness and hinder my ability to forgive. I certainly didn't need help to wallow in self-pity. It takes a very wise and courageous woman to say what I really needed to hear: "Hannah, you are sinning. You must forgive David." Each time I spoke with my dear friend, I had to carefully measure my words. Now, years later (and with my husband's consent) she does know some, but not all that I went through. She does not even know everything I have revealed in this book. I have only shared those things that are pertinent in encouraging her spiritual growth by seeing God's sovereignty and goodness demonstrated in my life.

I often hear women say things that are gossip in the form of a prayer request. Even a simple request like, "Please pray for us. We are going through a hard time right now," leads to gossip. So, save your prayer requests regarding your husband, for your biblical counselor, and the godly older woman who is mentoring you. Leave your peers out of it.

There may come a time when you can talk openly about it, but the goal must not be, "Look what I've gone through," but rather, "Let me share how good God is." For me the time to share has been obvious as I observed my own husband begin to share and counsel and help other men. The purpose should be to help other believers by testifying to God's sovereignty and lovingkindness. However, much time (years) should pass before doing so.

Getting God's Perspective

Betrayal, pain, and anger are all strong motivators. They powerfully urge you to tell anyone whom you think might be able to soothe the pain in your heart. But there are dangers. Indiscriminately seeking counsel from every sympathetic listener may only deepen the wounds and reinforce the bitterness. Real balm for your heart comes from the heart of God. Experiencing that balm can be aided by the love, comfort, and counsel of a woman who has herself walked with God and found Him faithful. The Bible studies in this chapter will help you learn discernment as you answer the question, "Who do I tell?"

Day One

The church is one of the wonderful blessings of salvation in Christ. Being part of the family of God means that we have a special place of comfort, security, and wise counsel when the suffering that is an inevitable part of life becomes a burden too heavy to bear alone. *"Blessed be the God and Father of the Lord Jesus Christ, the Father of mercies and God of all comfort; who comforts us in all our afflictions so that we will be able to comfort those who are in any affliction with the comfort with which we ourselves are comforted by God."*

Romans 15:14   Who is Paul talking about in Romans 15:14?

_____

The phrase *"able to admonish"* (NASB) means "able to give true counsel." Paul is stating that believers have a unique ability to give true counsel. Of course, he also describes two essential qualities of those believers. What two qualities does he note?

_____

_____

Those two qualities describe a believer that is living in Christ-like love for others (*"full of all goodness"*) and cultivating a thorough understanding of God's word (*"filled with all knowledge"*). This is the kind of person whom you need as your mentor.

1 Thessalonians 5:11 & 14   These two verses give the job description of a biblical counselor/mentor. What is a godly mentor to do?

_____

_____

_____

_____

_____

Day Two

Colossians 3:12-17   This Bible passage commands believers to develop certain qualities in their thoughts and behavior. The woman you choose as a mentor should have a life that substantially reflects these qualities. Of course, no woman will perfectly reflect all these qualities.

After each of the phrases below (taken from this passage) describe in your own words what an older Christian woman with this quality would be like.

"a heart of compassion" _____

_____

"kindness" _____

_____

"humility" _____

_____

"gentleness" _____

_____

"patience" _____

_____

"bearing with one another" _____

_____

"forgiving each other" _____

_____

"put on love, which is the perfect bond of unity" _____

_____

"Let the peace of Christ rule in your hearts" _____

_____

"be thankful" _____

"Let the word of Christ richly dwell within you" _____

_____

"with all wisdom teaching and admonishing" _____

_____

"with psalms and hymns and spiritual songs, singing with thankfulness in (her) heart to God"

_____

"do all in the name of the Lord Jesus Christ" _____

_____

(Also, review your answers from yesterday's Bible study.)

Developing a fruitful relationship with a woman like you just described will obviously be a rich blessing. Where can a woman like that be found? She will be found in a church that believes God's word, teaches God's word, and whose members continually encourage each other to live God's word. If you are not currently attending a church that meets that standard, you must make it your highest priority to find one. One place to look is the website for The Master's Seminary (www.tms.edu/AlumniByCityState.aspx). You might also go to the website for the Association of Certified Biblical Counselors (www.acbc.org). Click the "Find a Counselor" button to locate a certified biblical counselor in your area. He or she will be able to recommend a good church. Of course, there are other information sources, but these websites are a trustworthy place to start.

With the discernment you have gained the past two days, evaluate the women you have considered as a mentor and be proactive in pursuing the best choice.

Day Three

Discussing your husband's sin in his absence without his permission is gossip. Gossip destroys relationships. Though the temptation to talk to sympathetic friends will be strong, you must not, because destroying your husband's reputation will dishonor God and will drive your husband further away. Write down what you learn from these three scripture passages.

Proverbs 11:9 _____

_____

Proverbs 11:12-13 _____

_____

Proverbs 18:19 _____

_____

Day Four

Psalm 119:71-72   These verses make an astounding statement: *"It is good for me that I was afflicted, that I may learn Thy Statutes. The law of Thy mouth is better to me than thousands of gold and silver pieces."* Trusting God enough to obey His commands regardless of the circumstances is the sure gateway to blessing. Proverbs 3:8 promises us that it will bring healing and refreshment. However, sometimes the temptation to indulge our feelings is very strong. For instance, "sharing" with sympathetic friends what your husband has done may seem like the right thing to do. However, God's word says that women are not to be characterized by gossip.

Write down what you learn from these five Scriptures. The first one is answered for you.

2 Corinthians 12:20   In 2 Corinthians 12:20, gossip is listed with a group of seriously destructive sins. This indicates that gossip is also, like the others, a serious and destructive sin. Therefore, it is a sin that must be carefully avoided or seriously damaged relationships will result.

1 Timothy 3:11 _____
_____
_____

1 Timothy 5:13 _____
_____
_____

2 Timothy 3:1-5 _____
_____
_____

Titus 2:3 _____
_____

Day Five

Proverbs 31:10-31   describe "*an excellent wife.*" Verse twelve makes a very profound statement which is often overlooked.

> "*She does (her husband) good and not evil all the days of her life.*"

Think about what that statement is saying. All the days? Really? How about the days when her husband is sinning? Well ... This psalm is the oracle that King Lemuel's mother taught him. Do you think the King's mother was married to a perfect man who never sinned against her? Of course not. Doing good to her husband all the days of her life includes the days when his behavior was disgraceful and hurtful.

1 Peter 3:1-2   The opening phrase (*In the same way ...*) refers back to the previous paragraph (1 Peter 2:21-25). Thoughtfully read 1 Peter 2:21-25 and answer the question, "In <u>what</u> way?" The standard by which you are to evaluate your behavior toward your husband is Christ. You are told to walk in His footsteps. The example you are given is the Lord's response the night He was betrayed and crucified. During those hours of unspeakable suffering, what did Jesus do, and what did He not do?

While suffering, Jesus did not do 3 things: _____
_____

Instead, Jesus did 2 things: _____
_____

So when 1 Peter 3:1 commands you to respond to your husband in the same way as Christ responded to His persecutors, what does that mean in your particular circumstances?

_____
_____

According to 1 Peter 3:1-2, does your husband's sin remove your obligation to treat him with respect? _____

Does your husband's sin remove your obligation to try to live in accord with his wishes? _____

Would you being doing good to your husband by telling your friends and family about his sin? _____

Ephesians 5:33   This verse is the summary statement for God's teaching on marriage in Ephesians 5:22-33. As stated here, what is God's will for you in regard to your behavior toward your husband?

_____

The practical expression of real respect is to do your husband *"good and not evil all the days of (your) life."* It means to be chaste and submissive, and to choose to treat him in the way that brings him honor. Because of his sin, he may be more aware of his dishonor and his unworthiness. If so, your chaste and respectful behavior will be a powerful force pushing him toward full repentance and godly change. It is a wonderful experience to be used by God to bring lasting godly transformation in the life of another person.

Your Thoughts

_____

_____

_____

_____

_____

_____

_____

_____

_____

_____

_____

_____

_____

_____

_____

_____

_____

_____

_____

_____

_____

_____

Chapter 3
Anger and Grief

Hannah's Story

RAGE! My immediate reaction: flaming rage! I can remember wanting to find this woman and hurt her for taking my best friend and lover away; then flashing to, "How dare he!" But the Lord was gracious to me. He sovereignly gave me 30-40 minutes alone before my husband came home. The rage began to subside some, and then an overwhelming numbness came. I was able to function, to talk more calmly, and fix a meal for my children. It wasn't until late that night that the intense grief set in: uncontrollable sobbing; the realization that my heart was broken. I couldn't sleep. I would cry so hard I would hyperventilate. For several days, into weeks I would suddenly begin sobbing for hours, unable to breathe with the weight of pain and grief.

My young children could tell that something awful had happened. Mary reminded me that my children were watching to see how I would respond. So, at first I chose to keep going so they could see me obey God.

I asked myself, "What would a godly response look like? Hmm? Well …"

- Bringing David a glass of ice tea only an hour after finding out.

- Sleeping in the same bed with him.

- Respectfully asking David to get help (biblical help, not counseling from a psychologist, Christian or otherwise).

- Asking David to confess his sin to Christian family members who would support him with their prayers.

- Holding his hand that day.

- Initiating sexual relations that same week.

With Mary's support, I did these things. They were incredibly hard. I had to choose to ignore my emotions and do them only because it would please the Lord. Inside, my emotions were convulsing. I began to aggressively police David. I brooded on thoughts like, "What did I do?" "I'm not thin enough." "He doesn't want me." I am not sexually exciting enough." The journey had barely begun, and there was so far to go."

Getting God's Perspective

The questions Naomi asked herself were fueled by anger and grief. We will address these questions in later chapters. For now, let's focus on responding to anger and grief in a way that honors God.

Jesus manifested anger and grief when confronted with sin, rejection, or loss. Therefore, we know that anger and grief can be righteous and that at times of deep loss, it is healthy to weep. At those times, even in your sorrow, you must turn to the Scriptures to see your circumstance from God's perspective, become discerning at recognizing *sinful* anger, and protect yourself from the temptation to unleash *uncontrolled* anger.

Day One

You are grieving, and your grief is very real. You may feel abandoned and all alone. You want desperately to be comforted, but the one person who usually comforts you has betrayed you. Where can you turn to find comfort? Turn to the One who will never leave you or forsake you. Turn to the Lord. Mediate on Psalm 6:6-9.

Psalm 6:6-7   God has provided this example of David experiencing tremendous grief. God uses vivid word pictures to describe David's grief. Look at each word picture and describe in your own words what David is experiencing.

"I am weary with my sighing" _____
_____
_____

"Every night I make my bed swim" _____
_____
_____

"I dissolve my couch with my tears" _____
_____
_____

"My eye has wasted away with grief"
_____
_____

Based on the answers you just gave, do you think that David's grief was as intense as yours?

_____

Psalm 6:8-9
Even in his overwhelming grief David believed that God heard his weeping and received his prayers. He reminded himself of this truth and was comforted by it.

David knew that he was not alone and you can know that you are not alone. Write out a prayer telling the Lord about your grief and thanking Him for being with you and listening to you.

_____
_____
_____
_____
_____
_____
_____
_____
_____
_____

Day Two

Today I want you to spend time meditating on one particular aspect of God's character: God comforts His children when they are suffering.

Isaiah 66:10-14   In this passage God says that He will comfort His people the way a nursing mother comforts her baby. The allusion to a nursing mother and her baby is one that we as women can certainly understand. In verse 13, God says, "*As one whom his mother comforts, so I will comfort you.*" Describe how this verse gives comfort to you.

_____
_____
_____
_____
_____
_____

Isaiah 51:12   God reminds us that our comfort should be anchored in who He is. No matter what we are experiencing He promises to bring comfort. Write down some of the character qualities of God and make a note of how they give you hope and comfort.

Example: **God is just.** (Romans 12:18-21; 1 Peter 2:21-23) *It is comforting to know that He will right every wrong*

God is wise. (Romans 11:33-36) _____

_____

God is always with me. (Psalm 139) _____

_____

God is in control. (Romans 8:28) _____

_____

God is faithful. (1 Corinthians 10:13) _____

_____

2 Corinthians 1:2-5   God is the God of ALL comfort. God's comfort is abundant through Jesus Christ. Read 2 Corinthians 1:2-5 again. Verse 4 indicates that God uses other Christians to bring His comfort to us. In Chapter Two you were prompted to find a mature Christian woman to encourage and counsel you. If you have already established that relationship write her name below. If you have not, then follow through as soon as possible with the instructions you were given in Chapter Two.

_____

Day Three

Lamentations 3:19-32   Lamentations was written by the prophet Jeremiah in response to the brutal destruction of Jerusalem by Nebuchadnezzar. The brutality was unspeakable (Lamentations 2:1-22). Jeremiah's grief was overwhelming (Lamentations 3:1-18).

Lamentations 3:19-20   Jeremiah is brooding over his pain. What happened to Jeremiah as a result?

_____

_____

Lamentations 3:21-24   What is Jeremiah doing? Is this kind of recall spontaneous or a willful decision? _____

_____

Lamentations 3:21-24   In verse 21 Jeremiah says, "*This I recall to my mind, therefore I have hope.*" What is the connection between choosing to think about the character of God and having hope? _____

_____

Lamentations 3:21-32   Jeremiah mentions many truths about God. List those truths below and write down how each one encourages you. _____

_____

_____

_____

_____

_____

_____

_____

_____

Day Four

The Bible records many occasions when God's anger burned in response to sin. God's righteous anger is also on display at times in the life of Christ. Certainly your anger, if it is directed toward your husband's sin is a righteous anger. However, we are warned in James 1:20, *"The anger of man does not achieve the righteousness of God."* Today I want to help you evaluate your anger.

Proverbs 30:33   God gives us a vivid picture of the inevitable fruit of sinful anger. What does the passage say is the fruit of anger? What can you expect will happen if you allow your anger to affect the way you treat your husband?

_____

_____

Matthew 5:21-22   Jesus is very clear about the consequences of sinful anger. What does Jesus teach about unrestrained anger? _____

_____

_____

Self-focused anger is sinful. Prayerfully think through your emotions. Is your anger rooted in how your husband's sin has affected *you*? Write out a prayer confessing your sinful anger. Be specific about exactly which aspects of your anger are selfish. Ask God to forgive you for sinful anger. Tomorrow we will learn the godly response to anger.

_____

_____

_____

_____

_____

_____

Day Five

Today we will think about how to respond to anger in a way that honors God. Prayerfully read each Bible passage and then give thoughtful consideration to the teaching provided. As you do, be thinking about answers to the following questions:

1. What action or attitude will please God?

2. What have I been doing or thinking that is contrary to God's will?

At the end of today's Bible study you will be asked to write down your plans for making godly changes.

STEP ONE: Matthew 7:3-5. Step one in the godly response to anger is: Confess your own sin. Nothing that you have done in any way justifies your husband's sin. He alone is accountable for his sin. You are *not* responsible for what he did! However, as the Lord clearly states in Matthew 7:3-5, we must never allow another's sin to cloud our eyes in such a way that we are unable to see where we ourselves have sinned. Due to the interpersonal closeness of marriage, sinful responses are common for both the husband *and* the wife. These offenses tend to pile up, becoming a barrier that prevents the oneness God intended. A crisis point in the marriage relationship can be an opportunity to clear away old hurts and bring reconciliation that extends to every area through self-evaluation, confession, forgiveness, and godly change. Honoring God in this way will bring you unexpected joy. It will also profoundly affect your husband, and may even be the catalyst that brings him to full repentance.

Matthew 7:1-5   Read and meditate on Matthew 7:1-5. Spend the morning prayerfully making a "log list" (a list of your sins that have damaged your relationship to your husband). Tonight, after the kids are in bed, sit down with your husband, confess these sins without excuses, and ask him to forgive you. It will be hard … *very* hard! But the peace that will result will more than compensate for the struggle. Remember, God gives grace to the humble.

Did you notice that I just encouraged you to confess your sins without excuses? One way we make excuses is by giving a "Yes, but…" confession. What I mean by that is adding an accusation to your confession to justify what you had done. ("Yes, I yelled at you, but I wouldn't have if you hadn't provoked me!") Keep your confession pure and without excuse. ("I lost my temper and yelled at you. That was sinful. Would you please forgive me.?")

In what ways have you sinned against your husband? The following categories are provided to stimulate your thinking.

Finances _____

Withheld affection _____

Sex _____

Gossip _____

Being an ungodly example _____

Disrespect _____

Laziness _____

Gluttony _____

Other _____

Other _____

STEP TWO: Ephesians 4:22-32 and 1 Peter 2:19 – 3:2. Step two in the godly response to anger is: Check your response. How have you responded since you found out about his sin? God calls us to respond to undeserved suffering the way the Lord Jesus responded during his trials and crucifixion: no lashing out, no threats, no bitter malice. Our response must be characterized by kindness, tenderness, and forgiveness as we trust our heavenly Father to judge righteously. Take special note of Ephesians 4:30-32. God is calling you to *choose* to treat your husband with kindness rather than wrath.

STEP THREE: Romans 12:17-21. Step three in the godly response to anger is: Relax in the loving and omnipotent arms of God, and let <u>Him</u> deal with your husband. As we noted in 1 Peter 2:23, the response of the Lord Jesus to betrayal and suffering was to trust His heavenly Father to eventually make things right. The Lord is holy and faithful. Be assured that He will indeed make things right. You can trust Him. In fact, God is the avenger of sexual sin (1 Thessalonians 4:3-6). God says, *"Vengeance is Mine, I will repay, says the Lord."* You must not take your own revenge.

STEP FOUR: Ephesians 4:15, 29. Step four in the godly response to anger is: Use a gentle, loving tone of voice when talking to your husband. You need to be honest and transparent with your husband. He needs to understand your struggles. A word of caution here. This isn't a time to vent your feelings without restraint. You will communicate much more effectively if you speak the truth in love. *"A gentle answer turns away wrath, but a harsh word stirs up anger."* If you speak harshly, if he hears anger in your voice, he is likely to focus on your anger and become defensive rather than listening to what you are saying.

STEP FIVE: Ephesians 4:30-32 and Luke 17:1-4. Step five in the godly response to anger is: Be ready to forgive. Ephesians 4:32 commands that we forgive as God in Christ forgave us. What characterizes God's forgiveness? Isaiah 43:25 and Jeremiah 31:34 are very helpful in understanding God's forgiveness. Both passages state that God *chose* to forgive. Does His emotional response to our sin change? No, God hates our sin! He hates it so much that He poured out His wrath on His only begotten Son who bore our sin on the cross. God's hatred for our sin will never change. The wonderful thing about God's forgiveness is that He chose to forgive us in spite of our sin and His hatred for it. It was an act of His will; a choice. He has chosen to forgive, and He promises to lavish His grace upon us and bless us in every way imaginable. And so, in order to forgive as God forgave you, you must also choose to lavish grace and blessings on the forgiven one *in spite of* his sin. Specifically you must...

1. Choose to never bring it up again.

2. Choose not to brood over it.

3. Choose not to let it affect the way you treat him.

You can't wait until you feel like you want to forgive your husband. When you have been deeply hurt this kind of forgiveness is very difficult. Actually, it is *impossible* apart from the ministry of the Holy Spirit in your heart. That is why STEP SIX is so important.

STEP SIX: Ephesians 3:20-21 and Philippians 4:19. Step six in the godly response to anger is: Trust in God rather than your own strength. Jesus said, *"With people this is impossible, but with God all things are possible."* Be encouraged! Even though you may feel weak, God is strong. Though you may think you cannot do it, you can do it through the power of God. He is faithful. He will be with you and will strengthen you.

I will seek to please the Lord by making the following changes in the way I am relating to my husband:

_____
_____
_____
_____

Your Thoughts

_____
_____
_____
_____
_____
_____
_____
_____
_____
_____
_____
_____
_____
_____

Chapter 4
Endure

Hannah's Story

The first weeks seemed like a fog; it was as if life would never be the same. My husband was also my best friend. His betrayal left me feeling so alone. No one in our city knew about my situation, only our families, hundreds of miles away. At this point I felt hopeless. No hope means no motivation to go on. This was the beginning of my downward spiral towards wanting to die. Every day, countless times a day, I thought and planned ways to end my pain. ("I could crash my car into a tree, or take pills while they are at church.") Again and again I planned, but thoughts of my children whom God had entrusted to me kept me going one more day. During these seven to ten months I told no one I wanted to die. Finally I told Mary and my husband. This chapter, *ENDURE*, means so much to me. I was literally forcing myself to get up, shower, do my daily tasks, and love David all the while bearing pain so horrible I only wanted to scream, cry, but mostly stop and give up.

Asking you to endure may seem harsh, but *you have to!* Keep going. God is there, and in the end you will see his hand in it all.

Getting God's Perspective

Betrayal and loss can cascade into the deep hopelessness that Hannah described. But even if you have been spared such overwhelming despair, the wounds you have experienced are surely generating questions that leave you groping for something secure you can grasp. There is only one thing that offers complete security: the promises of God. You can rest in His promises because God is faithful and holy. I urge you to trust the One whose word gives hope that never disappoints. Hannah experienced the faithfulness of God as she chose to put one foot in front of the other, step by step, as she walked along the path that was set before her. This required many small decisions to do what God had called her to do. Each step she took led her closer to restoration and joy.

Day One

The deep hurt Hannah experienced led her into an emotional downward spiral that swept away her desire to live. Perhaps you can identify with her. Do you wish that you could die? Have such thoughts been pressing down upon you? Have you considered committing suicide? Hannah experienced this and yet told no one. I beg you not to make this mistake. If you have had *any* thoughts like this, immediately (today) take the following steps.

- Call you mentor/counselor and share these thoughts with her. Be very frank and transparently honest.

- If you have acquired the means to end your life (a drug, a weapon, etc.) give it to your counselor.

- If you have made a plan for how to end your life, explain it to your counselor in detail.

- Establish an agreement with your counselor that you will call her and talk to her every time you are tempted to carry out your plan. Promise her that you will not hurt yourself without talking to her first. Agree on another person you can contact if she is unavailable.

- Begin today memorizing and meditating on Psalm 139. Psalm 139 is a song with four stanzas (139:1-6, 7-12, 13-18, 19-24). Read the entire Psalm each day and meditate on the meaning of its truths to your life and circumstances. However, the memory work should be done one stanza at a time. Work on one stanza for several days until you can recite it word-perfect. Then add the next stanza, and then the next, and then the next until it becomes part of your very being. **Please memorize from the New American Standard version of the Bible.** (For your convenience Psalm 139 is printed below.)

NOTE TO THE COUNSELOR/MENTOR: If she does not bring this issue up on her own, you must love her enough to bring it up yourself. Be tender and sensitive, but do not shy away from discussing suicide and self-inflicted wounds. Be gentle but blunt. Your love and comforting counsel are key to helping her through this very painful experience.

Psalm 139:1-6

O Lord, You have searched me and known me.
You know when I sit down and when I rise up;
You understand my thought from afar.
You scrutinize my path and my lying down,
And are intimately acquainted with all my ways.
Even before there is a word on my tongue,
Behold, O Lord, You know it all.
You have enclosed me behind and before,
And laid Your hand upon me.
Such knowledge is too wonderful for me;
It is too high, I cannot attain to it.

Psalm 139:7-12

Where can I go from Your Spirit?
Or where can I flee from Your presence?
If I ascend to heaven, you are there;
If I make bed in Sheol, behold, You are there.
If I take the wings of the dawn,
If I dwell in the remotest part of the sea,
Even there Your hand will lead me,
And Your right hand will lay hold of me.
If I say, "Surely the darkness will overwhelm me,
And the light around me will be night,"
Even the darkness is not dark to You,
And the night is as bright as the day.
Darkness and light are alike to You.

Psalm 139:13-16

For You formed my inward parts;
You wove me in my mother's womb.
I will give thanks to You, for I am fearfully and wonderfully made;
Wonderful are Your works,
And my soul knows it very well.
My frame was not hidden from You,
When I was made in secret,
And skillfully wrought in the depths of the earth;
Your eyes have seen my unformed substance;
And in Your book were all written
The days that were ordained for me,
When as yet there was not one of them.

Psalm 139:17-24

How precious also are Your thoughts to me, O God!
How vast is the sum of them!
If I should count them, they would outnumber the sand.
When I awake, I am still with you.
O that You would slay the wicked, O God;
Depart from me, therefore, men of bloodshed.
For they speak against you wickedly,
And your enemies take Your name in vain.
Do I not hate those who hate You, O Lord?
And do I not loathe those who rise up against You?
I hate them with the upmost hatred;
They have become my enemies.

Search me, O God, and know my heart;
Try me and know my anxious thoughts;
And see if there be any hurtful way in me,
And lead me in the everlasting way.

Psalms 139:1-4   List all the things mentioned in this passage that God knows about you.

_____

_____

_____

_____

Psalm 139:5   This is a word picture: Visualize a father who loves and cares for his daughter by planting a protective hedge around her (NASB *"enclosed"*) and standing close by with his hand on her shoulder. What do the hedge and the hand tell you about God's involvement in your life at this moment?

_____

_____

_____

Psalm 139:7-12   In relationship to you, where is God right now?

_____

_____

Psalm 139:17-18   As you have seen in verses 1-16 King David is writing about how intimately involved God is in his life. Verses 17 and 18 reveal how frequently David is in God's thoughts. This intimate relationship with God is true of all Christians. (See Appendix A if you are unsure of your relationship with God.)

According to Psalm 139:17-18, how many times per day does God think about you?

_____

Day Two

Our hope is in God. You cannot control circumstances, but God can and does. You cannot anchor your happiness in the faithfulness of your loved ones. They will disappoint, but your heavenly Father is *always* faithful and will never disappoint. His loving presence is working all things toward an eternity in which you will experience immeasurable joy and security. Therefore, whenever your emotions send you spiraling downward in despair, turn to Him. His promises are vastly more sure than your emotions. What promises/assurances are given in the following Scripture passages. Use the blanks to write out the promises and record how those truths are relevant to your life today.

Psalm 32:10 _____

_____

Psalm 33:18 _____

_____

Psalm 34:15 _____

_____

Day Three

Hope comes through perseverance and the encouragement of the Scriptures. Re-read Hannah's story at the beginning of this chapter. Hannah persevered by occupying her thoughts with concern for her children and how much they needed her, and then working to meet those needs. This was the thing that carried her through those dark days. Hannah was being obedient to God's will. In Matthew 22:34-40 Jesus told us which commandments are most important.

"Teacher, which is the great commandment in the Law?" And (Jesus) said to him, "You shall love the Lord your God with all your heart, and with all your soul, and with all your mind. This is the great and foremost commandment. The second is like it, you shall love your neighbor as yourself."

God's will: Love Him and love others. We are to love with Christ-like love that is active, seeking to bless the loved one. Hannah looked beyond her own pain and despair and reached out to meet the needs of others (her husband and children), The Spirit of God within Hannah used her acts of service to rescue her.

Dear sister, look around you and see all those who would be harmed by your death and all those whom you could bless if you lived. Don't wait. Begin today to lavish loving-kindness on those whom God has placed in your life.

Romans 15:4-6   According to verse four, what two things combine to generate hope?

_____

Romans 15:4-6   Look up the words *"perseverance"* (NASB) and *"endurance"* (NIV) in a dictionary. Meditate on these definitions and then write down, in your own words, what verse four is encouraging you to do.

_____

_____

Hope arises out of despair when you fill your mind with the Scriptures, embrace God's promises, and actively obey His commands.

Romans 15:5 According to verse five, where does perseverance/endurance come from?

_____ . Therefore, prayer is an important aspect of perseverance. In the space below, write a prayer thanking your Lord for the encouragement of the Scriptures and pleading with Him to give you the strength and endurance to persevere.

_____

_____

_____

_____

_____

_____

Psalm 139 Take time working on memorizing Psalm 139:1-6. Then fill in the blanks below from memory. You have permission to make multiple copies of this page if the copies are used only to help you memorize the passage through repetition. The harder you work at this assignment, the greater will be the blessing.

Psalm 139, Stanza One

O LORD, You have _____ me and _____ me.

You know _____ and

_____.

You _____ my thoughts from _____.

You _____ my path and my _____

_____ ,

And are intimately _____ with _____

_____.

Even before there is a _____ ,

Behold, O LORD, You _____.

You have _____ me behind and before,

And_____.

Such knowledge is _____.

It is _____ , I cannot _____ to it.

Day Four

We have been talking about restoring hope even when your emotions cry out in despair. You have learned that hope comes from focusing on the faithfulness of God. You have found hope in the reality of His intimate presence and intense watch-care over you. And you have learned that hope comes through perseverance (doing what pleases God even when it is a struggle). Today I want you to meditate on the gospel itself: the good news that you have been (or can be) cleansed, given new life, and placed in a blessed relationship with God Himself that will continue throughout eternity.

Romans 5:1-11   These verses state the core truths of the gospel. They were written to be read by believers who have been saved from the wrath of God, forgiven of all their sins (past, present, and future), and given new life in Christ. If you are unsure of your salvation, please turn to Appendix A at the end of this book for a complete explanation of how to have your sins forgiven, be given new life in Jesus Christ, and gain assurance of your eternal destiny in heaven with Him.

Romans 5:1-5   Read Romans 5:1-5 and list, in order, the realities a child of God can expect.

1. Justification by faith

2. Peace with God

3. Grace

4. Tribulations

5. _____

6. _____

7. _____

8. The love of God

Romans 5:2   What are you to exult in? _____

Romans 5:3   What else are you to exult in? _____

There is a reason Paul placed these two seemingly unrelated things together: the glory of God and tribulations (i.e. suffering). Paul knew from experience that focusing on the glory of God had a dramatic impact on how he reacted when he encountered suffering.

Romans 5:6-11   Note the first word of verse six is *"For"*. *"For"* means *because*. It indicates that Paul is about to reveal the *reason* for his assertions that Christians should exult in the glory of God *and* in tribulation. According to Paul, you should exult in glory *and* tribulation because of what Jesus has done for you.

Romans 5:6 and 5:8   Before you were saved, you were a guilty sinner and helpless, with no defense before the judgment of God. Exultation begins with this thought: God is holy, but I am a sinner. God has no motive for saving me other than His incredible, undeserved love for me, and yet He willingly paid an unbelievably high price (the crucifixion of His beloved Son) to redeem me. I did NOTHING to deserve such amazing love!

Romans 5:9-11   Knowing that God the Father willingly redeemed us at a staggering cost, and that Jesus Christ willingly paid the price (His own death), you can have absolute confidence that you will escape God's just wrath and enjoy forever the benefits of reconciliation with Him. This is ample cause for exulting with joy even when experiencing a time of suffering. In Paul's letter to the Philippians, he expressed this in a very personal way.

"But whatever things were gain to me, those things I have counted as loss for the sake of Christ ... for whom I have suffered the loss of all things, and count them but rubbish in order that I may gain Christ ... that I may know Him, and the power of His resurrection and the fellowship of His suffering, being conformed to His death; in order that I may attain to the resurrection from the dead." (Philippians 3:7-11)

Write out a prayer expressing your heartfelt response to the realities and implications of what Jesus has done for you.

_____
_____
_____
_____
_____
_____
_____
_____

2 Corinthians 4:7-15   Based on what Paul mentions in these verses and in **2 Corinthians 11:23-33**, summarize the kinds of experiences Paul suffered through.

_____
_____
_____

2 Corinthians 4:16-18   Hope comes from a heavenly perspective. According to verse seventeen, what will be the ultimate outcome of the suffering you are currently experiencing?

_____

_____

2 Corinthians 4:16-18   Even though Paul endured many painful experiences, he did not lose heart. If you could talk to the apostle Paul, what counsel would he have for you according to verse 18?

_____

_____

_____

Day Five:

Hebrews 12:1   Yesterday you were encouraged to fix your hope on the glory that awaits you in Christ. It is important for you to occupy your mind with these thoughts rather than brooding over your present circumstances. In order to do that, you must place all your hope in the promises of God. However, sometimes, while we are suffering, we are tempted to ask, "Can I trust God?" Hebrews 12:1 answers that question with a strange sounding observation. It states that we have *"a great cloud of witnesses."* Whenever God's faithfulness is questioned, whose testimony should we seek? The author of Hebrews points us back to the Old Testament (summarized in Hebrews chapter 11) to hear the testimony of those who entrusted their lives to God and found Him faithful. These, the men and women of faith in the Old Testament, are the *great cloud of witnesses* referred to in Hebrews 12:1. They all give unanimous testimony: God is faithful.

Hebrews 11:32-40   Many people are mentioned in Hebrews 11:32-40 (named or unnamed). In verse 39 the writer states that they all *"gained approval through their faith."* And yet, in verses 32-38 their faith is not even mentioned. What *is* mentioned about these people in verses 32-38?

_____

All of these people had one thing in common: They believed God and acted courageously based on their trust in Him. And they all found Him faithful.

Hebrews 12:1-3   Fix your eyes on Jesus. He endured more suffering than you or I ever will. *"For the joy set before Him (He) endured the cross."* Did He find His heavenly Father faithful? _____

Will you find God faithful, if you place your hope in Him alone and trust Him with the outcome? _____

Dear sister, fix your eyes on Jesus. God will not disappoint you.

Psalm 139   Don't forget to work on memorizing Psalm 139 today. The more frequently you recite it, the more you will be blessed. Once you have perfected stanza one, move on to stanza two.

Chapter 5
Thoughts Like ...

Hannah's Story

Right away I began to struggle with thoughts like ...

"I'll never look like her."

"What did I do to push him away?"

"Why was I not enough for him?"

"What is she like that I'm not?"

"I'm not what he wants."

"He doesn't love me."

"If he loved me, he would have ..."

These thoughts seemed all-encompassing. My whole day swirled with brooding as I spiraled deeper into the pit of hopelessness and worthlessness. Meanwhile, David was receiving biblical counseling and being taught how to love me. My heart was confused. One moment I was consumed by hurt, anger, and grief. The next I was longing to be loved and I was missing my best friend.

Very late one evening, David got a call from work. He got up, quickly got ready, and left with no explanation. I waited for two hours and had no call. As the time passed my thoughts got the better of me. I began to go through his drawers, clothes, papers, etc. looking for a clue to his newest lover. By the time he came home, I was furious. I screamed and demanded to know why he hadn't called, where he was, and who he was with. He got defensive, and I assumed that his defensiveness meant that I was right. After all, I rationalized, he had lied to me for years. He told me he had been at work and offered to let me call his work supervisor to check on him. I was too infuriated to cooperate with his efforts to make peace. The next day we agreed to an uneasy peace, but I did not repent. In my mind, I had no reason to repent.

This incident occurred because I was looking for a fight. Seeds of bitterness were growing, and this was the fruit. David was attempting to do the things he should, but I was in no mood to respond rightly or even admit my bitterness. Even with Mary, I tried to hide my bitterness. I did not want her to see my sin.

Getting God's Perspective

Hannah's questions are not unusual. Perhaps you have asked some of these same questions or similar ones. Look closely at them. They are actually a strange mix of mental attacks that seem to be coming from contradictory perspectives. Some are self-depreciating. Some are tactical assessments. Some are prideful attacks on David. Together they paint a picture of a mental train wreck resulting from emotional overload. God's word gives us the explanation for Hannah's confusion: "*The heart is more deceitful than all else and desperately sick, who can understand it?*" (Jeremiah 17:9) "Deceitful" means to trick someone into believing something that isn't true. In the case of a brooding, injured heart, it is the brooding one who will become deceived. It is no wonder that Hannah was controlled by her imaginations. She was deceived by her own heart.

Jeremiah 17:9 ends with a question: "*Who can understand (your heart)?*" In verse ten, the Lord immediately answers Jeremiahs question: "*I, the Lord, search the heart.*" So, where should you go to seek answers to the questions twisting your heart? Should you trust your emotions, your reasonings, and your imaginations? No. Instead, let's look back to Jeremiah 17. In verses 5-8 God gives you both a warning and a promise of blessing.

> *Thus says the Lord,*
> *Cursed is the man who trusts in mankind*
> *And makes flesh his strength,*
> *And whose heart turns away from the Lord.*
> *For he will be like a bush in the desert*
> *And will not see when prosperity comes,*
> *But will live in stony wastes in the wilderness,*
> *A land of salt without inhabitant.*
> *Blessed is the man who trusts in the Lord*
> *And whose trust is the Lord.*
> *For he will be like a tree planted by the water,*
> *That extends its roots by a stream*
> *And will not fear when the heat comes;*
> *But its leaves will be green,*
> *And it will not be anxious in a year of drought*
> *Nor cease to yield fruit.*

Do you sometimes feel like that cursed man, alone in a desert wilderness? Perhaps you have allowed your heart to deceive you. You are *not* alone. The Lord is with you. Turn to Him. Trust in Him. Those who do, find a stream of life giving water that will refresh the spirit and restore fruitfulness and confidence. *(She) will be like a tree firmly planted by streams of water, which yields its fruit in its season, and its leaf does not wither; and in whatever (she) does, (she) prospers.*

Day One

Like a tree firmly planted by streams of water, it is very important for your thoughts to be drinking in God's precious word. Because the Scriptures are God-breathed, meditating on them brings you closer to Him. In preparation for today's study read Psalm 63:1-8.

Psalm 63:1   Verse one expresses David's longing for God. David compares his longing to being in a dry, weary land where there is no water. In your own words, describe the meaning that David is trying to communicate by the metaphors.

"my soul thirsts for you" _____

"my body longs for you" _____

"there is no water" _____

Psalm 63:2-8   David begins praising God when he takes his mind off his circumstances and remembers the truth about God. List the truths that David remembered about God.

_____

_____

_____

_____

_____

Psalm 63:6   Notice that David particularly mediates on God when he is lying awake in bed. At night time it is often difficult to think biblically about what you have been going through. Everything seems worse. At these times it is especially important to do what David did, meditate on the truth about God.

Day Two

One of my favorite passages is Proverbs 3:5-6. Remembering these verses has greatly helped me and others to trust in the Lord, especially when the counsel of friends, self-help books and our own thoughts are feeding our minds with the wisdom of the world. Take time now to read **Proverbs 3:5-8**.

Proverbs 3:5   At the beginning of this chapter we read from Jeremiah 17 and learned that our hearts are more deceitful than anything else. Proverbs 3:5 also warns us against leaning on our own thinking. What are we admonished to do instead? _____

Proverbs 3:6   We are told to acknowledge the Lord. Look up the word *acknowledge* in a dictionary. Based on the definition, what does it mean to acknowledge the Lord?

_____

_____
_____

Proverbs 3:6-7   We are told not to lean on our own understanding, not to trust our path, and not to be wise in our own eyes. So, what is it about God that you are to acknowledge?

_____
_____
_____

Proverbs 3:5-8   Write down the blessings you will receive if you trust in the Lord with all your heart and acknowledge that His way is better than your way and His wisdom is better than your wisdom?

_____
_____

Day Three

In Psalm 23 God uses the image of a shepherd to teach us about Himself so that we can more fully understand our God and the blessings He provides for His children. Read Psalm 23.

Psalm 23:1-3   King David begins by telling us that the Lord is like a shepherd. In these verses we are given a description of what the shepherd does for his sheep. Briefly describe what the shepherd is doing.

_____
_____
_____
_____

How are the things that the shepherd does to care for his sheep like the things that God does to care for you?

_____
_____
_____

Psalm 23:3   *"He guides me in the paths of righteousness for His name's sake."* A shepherd carefully chooses the right paths for his sheep to walk on. He doesn't want any of them to lose their footing or wander. The Lord will also guide you on the right path if you listen to His word.

Psalm 23:4   The rod and the staff were the weapons the shepherd used to protect his sheep. The sheep were safe as long as the shepherd was there to protect them. What banished David's fear and gave him comfort?

_____

Psalm 23:5-6 What blessings does David anticipate from the constant presence and protection of God?

_____

_____

_____

As David chose to trust God when walking through the valley of the shadow of death, God wants you to trust Him in your circumstances. Begin today actively looking for God's hand at work during this difficult time in your life. Record the ways God has been caring for and protecting you since you began working through this book.

_____

_____

_____

Day Four

1 Corinthians 13:1-13   What is love? God answers in 1 Corinthians 13 by telling us what love *does.* Every action arises out of our thoughts. Beside each statement from 1 Corinthians 13, write down one example of thoughts that would produce that manifestation of love. Two of the answers have been done for you as examples.

Love is patient "I will not stew when he fails to take out the trash."

Love is kind _____

Love is not jealous _____

Love does not brag _____

Love is not arrogant _____

Love does not act unbecomingly _____

Love does not seek its own _____

Love is not provoked "I will carefully consider the merit of what he says even when he is angry."

Love does not take into account a wrong suffered _____

_____

Love bears all things _____

Love believes all things _____

Love hopes all things _____

Love endures all things _____

Day Five

If you have been consumed with runaway thoughts, you may be thinking that there is no way you can control your thinking. Now is a good time to look to the Scriptures to see what resources God has provided for you when the situation looks impossible. Read **2 Peter 1:2-8**.

2 Peter 1:2 "Grace and peace"...When your thoughts are filled with turmoil, grace and peace are what you need. According to Peter, what brings grace and peace?

_____

2 Peter 1:19-21 Where do we go to gain knowledge of God and Jesus our Lord?

_____

2 Peter 1:3 God has granted you everything you need for life and godliness... everything! How do we gain access to these divine resources?

_____

2 Peter 1:4 By God's own glory and excellence, He granted to you precious and magnificent promises. What will be the outcome of you clinging to those promises?

_____

2 Corinthians 10:3-5 According to this passage is it possible for you to control your thoughts?

_____

Your weapons are divinely powerful as long as they are of God and not of the flesh. We must fight using the weapons God has given us and not give into our feelings.

Ephesians 4:22-24 When your mind begins to travel down the road of hurt and sin, you must stop yourself and get off that road. Make an immediate U turn so that you can get back on the right road. It is not enough to stop thinking destructive thoughts. You must replace those thoughts with thoughts that honor God. Or as Paul says in Ephesians 4, you must put off your old manner of life (thinking and behavior) and put on your new self which was created by God when you were born again. It is a conscious decision you must make. You must replace your destructive thoughts with thoughts like you wrote on your assignment from yesterday.

Begin today consciously choosing to replace the thoughts that are dragging you down. Every time those thoughts come to mind, open this book to your Chapter Five, Day Four homework and renew your mind with thoughts that honor both God and your husband. Read through those thoughts again now.

Your Thoughts

_____

_____

_____

_____

_____

_____

_____

_____

_____

_____

_____

_____

Chapter 6
Policing Everything

Hannah's Story

At this point I began to police everything I could. I questioned him about everyone he spoke to at work, church, home, on the phone, at the store, anywhere. I checked phone logs, went through his wallet, checked e-mails, and we discontinued our internet service. I went everywhere I could with him, even to get gas or pick up the dry cleaning. Every woman, even if she was a stranger or co-worker became an enemy. I began to critique how every woman was dressed, especially those at church, a place we couldn't avoid. I viewed each woman as someone I couldn't compete with. Even couples who wanted to be or were our friends seemed like possible enemies. I started mentally critiquing everything the wives wore: how tight, did underwear lines show? If they smiled or talked easily with David, or even if they had beautiful eyes or hair, or if they were a different height from me they became my enemies. So much so that I would give David a signal that let him know I was watching closely and he had a fine line to walk. He grew completely frustrated with this and eventually would decline invitations to be with friends or go to any functions.

I was so enveloped by self-pity and suspicion that I couldn't enjoy or even appreciate the changes that the Lord was making in David and the thoughtful ways he loved me almost every day. My mind was consumed by, "What if ..."

Getting God's Perspective

Hannah is right. Policing is caused by the combination of self-pity and suspicion.

Self-pity is the natural fruit of pride.

Did I just hear you say, "*NO WAY! My problem is not pride. I have poor self-esteem.*" Actually, you wouldn't experience self-pity unless you were convinced that you were being treated unfairly. In other words, you are whispering to your soul, "*I don't deserve this!*" If you will think about it you will realize that "*I don't deserve this*" is the exact opposite of low self-esteem. It is your pride reaffirming your superiority over your husband. Apart from the renewing influence of the Scriptures, we all tend to minimize our own sinfulness and rationalize, "*I don't deserve this.*" Thinking this way is understandable considering that in our day-to-day life we have only sinners with whom to compare ourselves. But we know that God is holy, and because we are not, His holiness makes humility an absolute obligation in His presence.

<u>Suspicion</u> is the backside of pride. It demeans the other person, refusing to believe anything positive about him. It reinforces self-pity by whispering, *"I have to watch him like a hawk. He is such a low-life jerk! I'm glad I'm not like that. He is lucky to have someone like me who is willing to stay with him. Of course, he doesn't even see how lucky he is."* I hope that if you recognize these thoughts as your own, the fact that they are written here will help you see how destructive they are. This kind of thinking poisons your mind and undermines progress toward your own healing and reconciliation with your husband.

Chapter Five begins with Hannah's out-of-control thoughts. Look back and read them again. Her thoughts are manifestations of self-pity (envy, self-depreciation, and anger). Self-pity is the breeding ground for other sins as well. Brooding self-pity leads to anger and bitterness. Anger and bitterness are acted out in a variety of destructive behaviors. In Hannah's case, she used her position as David's wife in a controlling way, policing everything David did. Note that she became consumed and enslaved to such an extent that she couldn't even see the hand of God at work. Once again, pride was deceiving her into thinking that by her policing she could control the situation.

But if you are God's child through faith in Jesus Christ, there is good news! Though God is opposed to the proud, He gives grace to the humble.
God loves His children with an everlasting love which motivates Him to cause all things to work together that they might be conformed to the image of His Son and experience the joy and blessing that the humble will know in fullest measure.
God will never give up on you. *"I am confident of this very thing, that He who began a good work in you will perfect it until the day of Christ Jesus."*
You can be absolutely confident that God will continue His work in you until He has perfected humility in you and blessed you beyond anything you could ask or think.

Day One

Psalm 37:1-8   In verse 7 we are encouraged to rest in the Lord and wait patiently for Him. Read Psalm 37:1-6 and make a list of the things you should be doing as you rest in the Lord.

_____

_____

_____

_____

Psalm 37:8   One of the blessings of resting in the Lord is being able to set aside anger and preoccupation with "fairness." That is what the Bible means when it says *"do not fret because of him"*. What does God say is the result of fretting?

_____

Fretting does not benefit you. It only drags you down, providing more opportunities to sin.

Day Two

God's standard is His own holiness, not "*Do the best you can.*" As our Lord Jesus said, "*You are to be perfect, as your heavenly Father is perfect.*"
By that standard we have no basis to boast and no basis to condemn others. Today you will apply that reality to your marriage. Pause to read **John 8:1-11.**

John 8:1-9   Today will be a role reversal for you. I want you to walk in your husband's shoes. Pretend, like the woman in the story, that you are the one who committed adultery. Read John 8:1-8. How would you feel if you had been the woman in this story?

_____

_____

_____

John 8:7-9   The story does not tell us what Jesus wrote on the ground. Use your imagination. In the light of John 8:7-9, what do you think he might have written?

_____

_____

Why do you think the on-lookers would not condemn you?

_____

_____

John 8:10-11   Again, pretend you are the woman in the story. How would you have responded when Jesus spoke those words to you?

_____

_____

John 8:7-11   Ok, it's time to reverse roles again. Pretend you are one of the people standing in the crowd, and pretend your husband is the woman. Would you be willing to walk away without seeking justice? Would you be willing to grant grace to the guilty one (your husband)? To do so would be Christ-like. It would also be hard.

Write out a prayer drawing from your answers to these questions.

_____

_____

_____

_____

_____

_____

_____

Day Three

Are you "policing" your husband? You may have heard of (or experienced) what is commonly referred to as "accountability partners." Accountability partners agree between the two of them to check up on commitments they have made to eliminate some sinful habit or pursue a godly one. Such partnerships are very helpful. However, they *are partnerships*. They are not one-sided vendettas to enforce the will of one upon the other. Wounded spouses are greatly tempted to take up such vendettas (what Hannah called *policing*). What causes policing? Policing results when love is replaced with suspicion, and trust is replaced by investigation. But behind all of that, policing is symptomatic of loss of trust in God's love and sovereign control. When we stop trusting God, we deceive ourselves into thinking that we must try to control anything that threatens us. For a betrayed wife, the object of control becomes her husband. So, you see, preoccupation with controlling your husband is faithlessness on your part. We, God's children, are called to a life characterized by love. God's will for you is to love your husband. If you are struggling with loving him as your husband, then love him as a brother in Christ. If you do not believe he is saved, then love him as a lost sinner. If you struggle with even that, love him as an enemy. Hear the words of your Lord:

> *I say to you, love your enemies, and pray for those who persecute you*
> *in order that you may be (daughters) of your Father who is in heaven.*
> *(Matthew 5:44-45, NASB)*

1 Corinthians 13:1-13   What is love? God answers in 1 Corinthians 13 by telling us what love *does*. Beside each statement from 1 Corinthians 13, write down one example of an action that would demonstrate love to your husband in a specific way. (**In Chapter 5 you did this exercise with your thought life. This time convert those thoughts to actions.**)

Love is patient _____

Love is kind _____

Love is not jealous _____

Love does not brag _____

Love is not arrogant _____

Love does not act unbecomingly _____

Love does not seek its own _____

Love is not provoked _____

Love does not take into account a wrong suffered _____
_____

Love bears all things _____

Love believes all things _____

Love hopes all things _____

Love endures all things _____

Love never fails _____

Perhaps your feelings are creating a barrier to loving your husband. Whenever you don't feel like loving him, refocus your mind by ...

Reminding yourself that your loving actions are an act of obedience to God out of a thankful heart. Remember, regardless of what your husband does, God is faithful.

Reminding yourself of the good qualities of your husband. Make a list of his good qualities to meditate on. In fact, do it right now. Make the list, put it in your purse, and take it out to meditate on it every time you need a boost to your commitment.

Day Four

The Lord loves reconciliation and unity. This is true even in the wake of sexual sin. In 1 Corinthians 5, Paul discusses a case of disgusting sexual immorality within the Corinthian congregation. In that case the guilty man was unrepentant and flagrant with his sin. However, later, following the man's repentance, Paul strongly admonishes the Corinthians to "*forgive and comfort him, lest somehow such a one be overwhelmed by excessive sorrow ... reaffirm your love for him ... in order that no advantage be taken of us by Satan; for we are not ignorant of his schemes.*"
 One of the ways Satan takes advantage of ruptured relationships is by tempting the victim to succumb to fear, suspicion, and self-pity. If you succumb to these temptations, it will affect the way you treat your husband, and this will further injure your already hemorrhaging relationship.

1 Peter 5:6-10   Read and meditate on 1 Peter 5:6-10.

1 Peter 5:6-7   Verses six and seven are a single thought. The allusion to God's mighty hand is in connection with His care for you. Review Psalm 139. (By now you should be able to easily recite it word-perfect.) Repeat 139:5-6.

Thou hast enclosed me behind and before,
And laid Thy hand upon me.
Such knowledge is too wonderful for me;
It is too high, I cannot attain to it.

Psalm 139:5-6 paints a word picture with the same meaning as 1 Peter 5:6-7. Why is it comforting to humble yourself under the mighty hand of God?

_____

_____

1 Peter 5:6-8   You are commanded to be sober and alert.

Sober: serious, solemn, and purposeful.

Alert: watchful and vigilant while guarding against surprise or danger,

2 Corinthians 2:7-11 and 1 Peter 5:8 warn you about Satan taking advantage of times when you are fearful, suffering, and/or unforgiving. Are you experiencing any of these temptations regarding your husband? What actions can you take to ensure that you are sober and alert to these three dangerous circumstances? Your answers should be in the following format: **When I _____, I will _____.**

Example: **When I** *am fearful and am tempted to police my husband,* **I will** *recite Psalm 139:5-6 and remind myself that God is protecting me.*

Fearful _____

_____

Suffering _____

_____

Unforgiving _____

_____

1 Peter 5:10   Peter reminds you that the God of all grace is acting on your behalf and will bring about a glorious outcome <u>regardless of whether your husband repents or not</u>. You may feel weak and helpless, but ultimately you will overcome, though not by means of your own strength. Who will perfect, confirm, strengthen, and establish you?

_____

Day Five:

I realize this chapter has been hard on you. I have asked you to do many hard things, including self-evaluation and confession. May the Lord richly bless you for following through. Today we will stop to assess your progress.

2 Corinthians 3:17-18   God is at work in your life. Are you aware of it? Read 2 Corinthians 3:17-18. The mirror Paul refers to is God's word, the Bible. (Read 3:14-16 to confirm this.)

For weeks now you have been looking into that mirror (God's word). According to 2 Corinthians 3:18, what has the Holy Spirit been doing during this time in His word?

_____

_____

_____

Spend time in prayer thanking God for all His loving activity on your behalf.

REMINDER: Don't stop working on memorizing Psalm 139. Keep reviewing stanzas one and two so you can easily recite them word-perfect. Now add stanza three. It is very helpful to write it down from memory. Writing it on paper has the effect of more indelibly writing it into your memory.

Your Thoughts

_____

_____

_____

_____

_____

_____

_____

_____

_____

_____

_____

_____

_____

_____

_____

_____

_____

_____

_____

_____

_____

_____

Chapter 7
Being Discreet
Who to Talk to and When

Hannah's Story

Once again I was confronted with the opportunity to tell a new friend about my hurt. Louise is new into our lives. In a very friendly conversation, she asked me questions of how long we had been married, how we met, how we were saved, and our views on courtship and dating. I spoke freely recalling the happy details of our dating and marriage. I gave my testimony, leaving out my current and past struggles. Louise asked me how long David had been saved, and when I responded less than a year, she was curious to know the circumstances. Here was a prime opportunity for me to share my pain with a godly lady. It was also an opportunity to love David and honor God by exercising discretion. Thankfully, I pondered my words and responded that David was saved through a trial the Lord recently brought us through. Louise was gracious and did not push to learn more.

Getting God's Perspective

There are many passages of scripture that admonish us to confess our sins, but the key word in that admonition is the word "our". Confession is the sole responsibility of the sinner. As you learned in Chapter Two, talking about the sins of someone else when they are not present and without their permission is gossip. Gossip often *destroys* relationships, but God is honored through reconciliation.

This is now the third time Hannah and I have encouraged you to be careful to talk about your husband's sin with only those who have a biblical need to know. In most cases, you must only discuss his sins with those whom he authorizes (your counselor, your mentor, etc.) Though the temptation to seek out a sympathetic ear is great, you must honor God by exercising self-control and discretion.

Hannah chose to be discrete, and God, in His wisdom, blessed her with reconciliation. God always gives what is best to each one of His children. However, that will sometimes include sorrow and suffering. Hannah's husband eventually repented and was restored, but this will not be the case with every sinning spouse. Therefore, God gives us guidance for that circumstance as well. In this chapter you will answer the question, "What does biblical discretion require of me if my husband does not repent?"

Day One

God hates divorce and loves reconciliation. Your husband's sin has given you a wonderful opportunity to give God pleasure by pursuing reconciliation. However, full reconciliation requires repentance by both parties resulting in cleansing of the relationship. In earlier chapters we have focused on your own repentance and cleansing. If you thoroughly followed through, I am confident that you are experiencing the blessings of a clear conscience and a refreshed intimacy with the Lord.

Hopefully, your husband has also repented. However, if he has not, God has additional work for you to do. The Bible passage on which you will meditate today, **Galatians 6:1-4**, will both define your mission and show you how to accomplish it.

NOTE: The commands of Matthew 18:15-18 and Galatians 6:1-4 are given to Christians in regard to dealing with _other Christians_ who are committing ongoing sin. If your husband is an unbeliever, this passage does not apply to him. You can, however, respectfully appeal to his conscience to discontinue his sin.

Galatians 6:1   What is your mission?

_____

Galatians 6:1-4   What specific actions could you take that would help restore your husband?

_____
_____
_____
_____
_____

Galatians 6:1-4   If your husband has not yet repented, you have a responsibility to encourage him to repent. Repentance is a gift from God (Acts 5:30-31, 11:17-18), therefore, your first step is to pray, pleading with God to grant repentance to your husband. Then you must go to him in private and plead with your husband to repent. According to Galatians 6:1-4, what must be communicated by your demeanor, body language, words, and tone of voice as you plead with him?

_____
_____

Galatians 6:1-4   Gentleness and humility will probably not come naturally while confronting your husband regarding his sin. In anticipation of this, Paul gives you advice on how to prepare your heart for this encounter. Write down specifically what you will do to utilize each of the strategies mentioned by Paul to ensure a gentle, humble demeanor during the encounter with your husband.

In a spirit of gentleness _____

_____

Looking to yourself _____

_____

Bear (his) burdens _____

_____

Remind yourself that you are nothing _____

_____

Bear (your) own load _____

_____

Day Two

Matthew 18:15-16   Who is speaking in Matthew 18:15-20? _____

Note that the Lord commands that sin be discussed *in private.* This is consistent with what you learned in chapters one and two of this book. Also note that no time limit is given for how long you should continue to appeal to him. Do not be in a hurry. This initial step may take several attempts, and progressing to step two (Matthew 18:16) should only be done when you are convinced that further effort on your part will be fruitless.

Remember what you learned yesterday: Every time you discuss your husband's sin with him, it must be done with gentleness and humility.

Your assignment for today: Re-read Chapter Two in this book.

Day Three

Matthew 18:16-17   If your humble efforts to encourage your husband to repent have been fruitless, and you are convinced that further effort may become an irritant rather than a blessing, you must obey the Lord and find one or two others to help you. According to **Matthew 18:16**, what will be their role?

_____

Note that they are to be objective. They are not there to back you up. They are there to determine the truth. Based on the first phrase of **Matthew 18:17**, what responsibility do they have in addition to fact finding?

_____

In order for these people to function effectively, they must be individuals whose lives are deserving of respect. I believe that the best choice is someone from your church whom you both respect. They must be devout believers with a good functional knowledge of the Bible. Someone with a good relationship with your husband could best fulfill this role. Get out your church membership roster and write down the names of those who meet these qualifications. Your mentor may be able to help you make this important choice.

_____

_____

_____

_____

Day Four

Matthew 18:17-20   When private admonition fails, and semi-private reinforcement has no effect, the unrepentant sinner must be reported to the church. This is for the benefit of the sinner and the protection of the church. When Jesus said, "Tell it to the church," functionally this meant to tell it to the church leaders. Once this is done, it becomes their responsibility to make biblical decisions and take biblical actions. The important principle for you to remember is that this is *NOT* to be done until private confrontation has failed. You are not to tell anyone, not even your pastor, until you have been obedient to Matthew 18:15-16.

Matthew 18:21-35   Immediately after teaching us how to deal with an unrepentant sinner, Jesus taught about forgiveness. These two subjects are inextricably tied together. All the while we are obediently encouraging repentance, our heart must be eager to forgive.

Matthew 18:32-34   In this parable, the king became very angry with his unforgiving servant. What was he angry about? Why did this anger him so?

_____

_____

_____

Matthew 18:23-34   The wicked servant had been forgiven an enormous debt. This is true of every believer. Paul expresses it this way.

> *He made you alive together with Him, having forgiven us all our transgressions, having canceled out the certificate of debt consisting of decrees against us and which was hostile to us; and He has taken it out of the way, having nailed it to the cross.*

Considering the graciousness of God in forgiving ALL of your sins, what should be your response when you are sinned against? What should be your response to your husband? (Consider The Lord's Prayer, Matthew 6:9-15.)

_____

_____

_____

Day Five

God has forgiven all your sins. All of them! Even the ones no one else knows about. Even the ones you won't even acknowledge to yourself. The proper response (the *required* response) is to become a forgiving person. Forgiveness should become such an intrinsic part of a Christian's character that it becomes the automatic reflex response whenever she is sinned against. However, sometimes the sin is so offensive and hurtful that forgiveness is very difficult. Sexual sin is like that. Does God really require you to forgive when the sin is so repugnant? Yes, He does. In fact, He gave us an example in the Bible. In 1 Corinthians 5, God recorded an incident in the life of the Corinthian church. One of the church members was having an on-going sexual relationship with his father's wife, and he wasn't even hiding it! What's more, he showed no signs of repentance or a willingness to stop sinning. As a result, God required that he be excommunicated (removed and isolated) from the church. This is an example of one of those rare cases when every member of the church had to be informed of the man's sin. However, even in this, there is no license to gossip or spread this knowledge beyond the church family. Even in such an extreme case, discretion in who you tell is still required.

The story does not end there. It picks up again in 2 Corinthians 2:4-11.

2 Corinthians 2:4-5   Note the phrase, "*in order not to say too much.*" What does this tell you about the Apostle Paul's commitment to discretion when speaking about someone else's sin?

_____

_____

2 Corinthians 2:7-   What three things were the church members commanded to do for this man who had flagrantly committed a hardhearted, disgusting sin but had now repented?

_____

_____

2 Corinthians 2:7   What reason did Paul give for forgiving and comforting him?

_____

_____

Jesus taught that unforgivness was a stumbling block to the one who remained unforgiven.[1] In 2 Corinthians 2:7, Paul mentions one of the ways this can happen. When someone becomes overwhelmed by excessive sorrow, the resulting hopelessness destroys motivation to godly change. The hope that was generated

---

[1]   Luke 17:1-10. Jesus also warned that it would be better to tie a millstone around your neck and be thrown in the sea than to be a stumbling block.

by repentance is dashed, and his initial commitments to godly living fall away unfulfilled. So you see, if you choose to withhold forgiveness from your husband, you are violating God's will and undermining your husband's spiritual progress.

Right now, settle this issue with God. Forgive your husband from your heart and commit to treating him in ways that will comfort him and reaffirm your love for him.

List at least ten things you can do to comfort and reassure your husband.

_____

_____

_____

_____

_____

_____

_____

_____

_____

_____

Your Thoughts

_____

_____

_____

_____

_____

_____

_____

_____

_____

_____

_____

_____

_____

_____

_____

_____

_____

_____

Chapter 8
The Fruit of Bitterness

Hannah's Story

1. Reliving the Pain

At this point I am going through the motions of loving David, trying to forgive him by putting on love. There is one key problem hindering me. One that keeps rearing its ugly head and, if left unconfessed and unchecked, *will* inhibit my ability to forgive David. What is it? Very simply: reliving the day I found out about the other woman, the content of the e-mails, and my feelings of inadequacy when compared to the porn star I have convinced myself David really wants. I easily rationalize that I need to review the details of the past to prepare for future "what ifs" and be aware of what to watch for. Besides (I tell myself), I must not forget what David did. If I don't remember my pain, no one will.

2. Believing I'm Trash

David has started to see a change in me. He says I am not so bitter, but inside I feel like screaming, "All I am is *TRASH* to you! I want to die. I am worthless." I want to make him hurt like I am hurting, so I say, "Was it worth it? Was she, the excitement, the erotic chats, worth losing me?" In my mind I answer my own questions: "Yes! Because if he loved me, wanted me, or if I was enough, *she* would not have been needed." I repeated these same answers to myself again and again.

On other days, I ask, "Why? Why did you hurt me?" As if anything he could say would even begin to soothe my crushed and bleeding heart.

I am hiding the fact that I want to commit suicide to end my constant hurting and to thereby make him suffer. He seems to have been rewarded with encouragement from parents and counselors who appreciate the changes he has made. He sinned, ripped out my heart, demolished our relationship and trust, and yet it is I who suffer.

3. That's Too Hard to Believe

The last time I talked to Mary about my bitter thoughts she reminded me of the need to replace those thoughts with thoughts that honor God and honor David as well. She encouraged me to dwell on the truth that David was loving me *now*. I almost threw up! I could not accept that or even say that, much less believe that. "He loves me?!" Immediately revulsion would occur. How could it be true? He wouldn't have done that if he did.

I had to find a way to change my thinking. I finally gave in and began to do as Mary had instructed me to do: I began to dwell on the little acts of love David did for me, such as making the coffee in the morning and cleaning up the kitchen in the evening. Those were tangible acts of love that I could dwell on. Every time I had those bitter, depressing thoughts, I would remind myself of his acts of love. Gradually things changed. Instead of wanting to die a thousand times a day, these thoughts came only perhaps once each week. Instead of thinking, "I am worthless" 20,000 times a day, only a few. Several weeks went by. I still didn't believe, but I kept adding to my *Ways David Loves Me* list. The longer I persevered in replacing my thoughts, the greater was the change. Eventually I began to think, "Perhaps it's not too hard to believe. David may love me."

4. No One Will Remember

I knew that I was bitter. I knew that it was sinful. I had confessed it to God and sought His forgiveness, but I resisted confessing it to David and Mary. I knew the reason. I knew what held me back. It was fear. It may seem strange to someone who has never been crushed like this, but I felt that if I didn't hold on to this, no one would remember. I wanted people to acknowledge what happened to me, and not allow him to go unpunished. How could I accept the whole thing being forgotten? Was all this horrible pain for me to bear in silence, while David comes away with the reward of a faithful wife?

Getting God's Perspective

Years ago, when I lived in Georgia, my husband worked tirelessly to eradicate a weed growing in our yard. We don't know the real name for this weed, but it was so destructive that my husband called it "the devil weed." My husband would pull it up, and it would grow back. He would poison it, and it would grow back. He finally resorted to digging out the roots. That was effective, but he had to be constantly on guard for any new "devil weed" to appear. It was only in this way, that he was able to protect our grass from destruction. Bitterness is a like that "devil weed." It quickly multiplies, spreads, and chokes out a loving relationship that has been carefully cultivated for years. Its roots must be dug out and we must always be watchful for its return.

The roots of bitterness are unforgiveness and brooding over a real or imagined offense. As you see in Hannah's story, the fruit of bitterness can be manifested in many ways.

Day One

Bitterness causes harm both to you and to those around you. Today we will look at the harm it can do to others.

Hebrews 12:14-15   The first word in this passage is *pursue*. The Greek word that was translated *pursue* is a very aggressive word. It means to run something to ground as a lion would chase his prey with intention to kill. In Hebrews 12:14, God commands you to pursue peace. What <u>kinds</u> of things would a person do to aggressively pursue peace with someone with whom they are in conflict?

_____

_____

_____

_____

List five specific things you will do to aggressively pursue peace with your husband?

_____

_____

_____

_____

_____

Hebrews 12:14   *"Pursue peace with all men and the* **sanctification** *without which no one will see the Lord."* This verse may strike you as difficult to understand. "Sanctification" means to set someone (or something) apart for God's exclusive use. In the ultimate sense, God does this for every believer at the moment of salvation. In another sense, each believer must strive to make this a practical reality in her life by putting off selfish desires and sinful habits and diligently developing godly habits and fostering godly character. Both of these aspects of sanctification are manifestations of the Holy Spirit's activity as He transforms believers in Christ-likeness. All true believers manifest both. Therefore, there is no such thing as a believer who is not sanctified (type one) and not being sanctified (type two). Therefore, no one will be saved without sanctification. The admonition to *"pursue ... sanctification"* indicates that the second type (the striving type) is in view here. If you have been saved, you have been set apart for God's exclusive use, and you must make living for Him alone the central focus of your life. Of course, your marriage is a huge part of your life, and therefore, striving for Christ-likeness in your marriage is an essential aspect of your sanctification.

Hebrews 12:15   *"See to it that no one comes short of the grace of God..."* The author of Hebrews repeatedly warns his readers of the danger of believing they are saved when they are still trusting in something other than the grace of God available through faith placed completely and exclusively in Jesus Christ. Saving faith trusts in Christ alone, not Christ plus some good work (such as baptism, church membership/attendance, humanitarian service, financial giving, etc.). Thus, a person who attempts to add any of her own accomplishments to God's grace in Christ *comes short of the grace of God.* It is also true that believers are to imitate God.[2] Therefore, we are to extend grace to others, just as God, in Christ, lavished grace on us.[3] It would be totally inconsistent for someone to pursue peace and sanctification (verse 14) while withholding grace from someone else.

Are you trusting in anything other than faith in Christ alone for your salvation? (faith plus church membership, faith plus good works, etc.)

_____

_____

Are you refusing to be gracious to someone even though God has been so gracious to you? _____

_____

Hebrews 12:15 The seed that germinates and puts out roots of bitterness is _NOT_ the hurtful behavior of the other person. No one can *make* you bitter. The seed that creates bitterness is a choice you make: refusal to forgive. If you harden your heart against your husband, you are planting the seed of bitterness. If you continue to brood over his sin, rehearsing it over and over, you cultivate the seed, nourishing it with water, fertilizer, and heat. Under such conditions, it is predictable that a root of bitterness will germinate and grow.

Hebrews 12:15   *"See to it that ... no root of bitterness springing up causes trouble, and by it many be defiled."* Give careful thought to your thought habits. Do you allow your thoughts to dwell on what your husband did and the pain he caused? How have the resulting intense emotions negatively affected your close relationships?

Husband _____

_____

Children _____

_____

Extended family _____

_____

Church _____

_____

Friends _____

_____

Day Two

The fruits of bitterness are poisonous. It is important that you learn to recognize

---
2   Ephesians 5:1-2
3   Ephesians 1:7-8, 4:30-32

them. Read this chapter's segment of Hannah's story again, and as you read look for the thoughts, attitudes and behaviors her bitterness produced. Record your findings below.

1. Reliving the Pain

_____
_____
_____
_____
_____

2. Believing I'm Trash

_____
_____
_____
_____
_____

3. That's Too Hard to Believe

_____
_____
_____
_____
_____

4. No one Will Remember

_____
_____
_____
_____
_____

Day Three

Bitterness produces poisonous fruit. One of the most common fruits is the desire for vengeance. The desire for vengeance motivates all manner of creative actions designed to make the guilty person miserable. But once that desire is realized, once the misery level of the guilty one has been pushed to the limit, what has actually been accomplished? Does vengeful success bring happiness or any other benefit? No. Bitter revenge only intensifies misery for everyone it touches (especially the bitter one) without achieving any tangible benefit. But is the victim of hurtful behavior helpless? Again, the answer is, "No." God has given His injured child a weapon of incredible power. Read **Romans 12:17-21** to discover it.

Romans 12:17-21   Organize the teaching of Romans 12:17-21 by filling in the following chart. List all the things you are told not to do in the column titled "Never ..." List all the things you are commanded to do in the column titled "Instead ..."

Never ...	Instead ...

Romans 12:17-21   Notice the combative language in this passage (*"pay back" "revenge" "enemy" "overcome"*). It is apparent that God wants you to make an all-out attack on the problem.

What action are you to take? _____

What weapon are you to use? _____

List one "burning coal" (i.e. loving act) you can heap on your husband's head today, and six additional "burning coals" you can heap on his head this week. Make a commitment to God to do these things at the first opportunity.

Today: _____

This Week: _____

_____

_____

_____

_____

Day Four

Today meditate on each of the following passages and record what each one says you should do in response to your husband. Give an example of what that will look like in application to your current circumstances.

1 Peter 3:8-10 _____
Example: _____

1 Thessalonians 5:15 _____
Example: _____

Romans 12:14 _____
Example: _____

Matthew 5:39, 43-45 _____
Example: _____

Day Five

The Epistle to the Philippians was written to a very fruitful, faithful church. However, like every other church, it was not without problems. For instance, in Philippians 4:2-7 Paul gave instructions to provide counseling for two women who were not getting along. In verses four through seven, Paul provided specific counsel on how to overcome interpersonal conflict.

Philippians 4:4-6   List the five specific actions that Paul encouraged them to take.

1. _____

2. _____

3. _____

4. _____

5. _____

Philippians 4:5   In the middle of his counsel, Paul reminded them that "the Lord is near." The Lord is near in two ways. (a) He is near each and every moment of every day. He is with you and in you. He is protecting you and empowering you. You learned this in your meditation on Psalm 139. (b) The time of Christ's return to earth in glory is also near. When He returns, He will restore justice and reward His children.

How should these truths motivate you to follow Paul's counsel?

_____

_____

_____

Philippians 4:4-6   *"Rejoice in the Lord always ... with thanksgiving ..."* These two admonitions are closely related. When in the midst of an interpersonal conflict, thanksgiving does not come naturally. Thanksgiving comes from a heart that is rejoicing in the Lord. What can you be thankful for regarding the current situation within your marriage?

_____

_____

_____

_____

_____

_____

Philippians 4:6   This verse encourages you to be anxious for nothing. Of course, that includes the uncertainties you are currently facing in your marriage. What is it about God and your relationship to Him that enables you to be free of anxiety?

_____

_____

_____

_____

Philippians 4:7   Does the peace of God seem unattainable? Such feelings are not surprising. After all, this passage explicitly states that the peace of God surpasses all comprehension. The truth is that peace is not out of reach. It is founded on faith in God and His promises, and it is attained by conformity to the wisdom of God revealed in verses four through six. Take this opportunity to spend time in prayer. It will also be helpful to review your memory work (Psalm 139).

Your Thoughts

_____

_____

_____

_____

_____

_____

_____

_____

_____

_____

_____

_____

_____

_____

_____

_____

_____

_____

Chapter 9
Perseverance

Hannah's Story

More than once I have been counseled to endure. Now I am being counseled to persevere. What does that mean? Answer: Never give up! What does that look like? At first I sought ways to please David. I bought him his favorite candy bar. I added his favorite meal to our weekly menu. But something was missing. I realized I needed to change my focus. Now, in addition to doing things to please David, I spent time praying for God to heal our marriage, to give me joy in serving David, and to give me perseverance: perseverance to work hard at growing in my relationship to David, and more importantly, in my relationship with the Lord. I gratefully acknowledge that the Lord has answered those prayers. Every day contains joy, and though we sometimes stumble, our progress is undeniable.

Getting God's Perspective

Again and again I have pointed you to promises and principles in the Bible and noted that these can be confidently applied to your life if you are a child of God. The child of God has been given new life (radically changed in their heart and given eternal life) and has the Spirit of God dwelling in them. Because of this, God's child can face the future with confidence and joy regardless of circumstances. **Philippians 1:6** says the following about God's children.

> *I am confident of this very thing, that He who began*
> *a good work in you will perfect it until the day of Christ Jesus.*

This means that God is actively working in the life of each of His children to bring about godly change. This change will progress until death or the day that Jesus Christ physically returns in the sky to take all of God's children to be with Him for eternity. On that day, He will instantaneously bring this process to perfection. Once this process is begun, the end result is completely assured (i.e. perfection).

> *For the gifts and the calling of God are irrevocable.*
> *(Romans 11:29)*

This process of godly change in the life of a true Christian (called *progressive sanctification*) is particularly important when it comes to perseverance. In the past, you may have resolved to make some change (lose weight or eliminate a bad habit, for instance). You undoubtedly worked at it faithfully for a while, but as time went on your enthusiasm waned, and you gradually quit trying. In other words, you failed to persevere.

If you are to experience the full blessing that comes through obedience to God's word, you must persevere. For that to happen, you need God's help. You need Philippians 1:6 (quoted above) to be true of you. If you have not yet used *Appendix B* at the back of this book to learn how to be sure you are God's child, do so now.

Day One:

Read and meditate on **Romans 5:1-6**.

Romans 5:3-4   Good News! If you are a child of God, God will use your current difficult circumstances to produce perseverance in you. According to verse 4, what will flow out of perseverance!

PERSEVERANCE → _____ → _____.

Does that sound good? A heaping helping of hope would taste good right now, wouldn't it?

Romans 5:3   Tribulation (difficult circumstances) produces perseverance which results in godly character changes and eventually leads to hope. As a result (according to verse three), what should be your attitude toward the difficulties you are experiencing due to your husband's sin?

_____

_____

Of course, you are not to rejoice that your husband sinned. However, you *should* be rejoicing in the knowledge that God is going to produce very good fruit in your life as you respond to your husband's sin in the way that pleases God.

Romans 5:1-2   Even more important, if you are a true Christian, you have "peace with God." This means that you no longer need to fear His wrath. Even though you are a guilty sinner, you are at peace with Him. This is because He has graciously forgiven you, given you a new life and many precious promises, including the privilege of a loving relationship with Him now and the surety of an eternity in His presence, enjoying His glory. Why should this cause you to rejoice today? How should this affect the way you respond to today's difficulties?

_____

_____

_____

How does anticipating spending eternity in the presence of the glory of God affect your commitment to persevere in consistently doing the things you have learned through the Bible studies in this book?

_____

Day Two

2 Peter 1:5-8   You have a part to play: diligence.

Note that verse five begins with *"Now for this very reason..."* Of course, to find out what reason Peter is referring to, you will have to read the previous sentences (verses 2-4).

According to 2 Peter 1:2-4 we have the following reasons to be *"applying all diligence."*

2 Peter 1:3   God has granted to us everything pertaining to life and godliness.

2 Peter 1:3-4   By His own glory and excellence, god has granted to us His precious and magnificent promises.

2 Peter 1:4   You have become a partaker of the divine nature.

2 Peter 1:4   You have escaped the corruption that is in the world.

2 Peter 1:5-8   Write out in sequence, one below the other, each of the qualities that you are to diligently add to your life.

_____

_____

_____

_____

_____

_____

_____

_____

Note the presence of *perseverance* in the list. You have gained much knowledge as you progressed through this book. Perseverance is essential to bearing the very best fruit.

2 Peter 1:8   *"For if these qualities are yours and are increasing, they render you neither useless nor unfruitful in the true knowledge of our Lord Jesus Christ."* I'm sure you know from experience that being useful and fruitful is a major contributor to happiness. I assure you that when usefulness and fruitfulness is in the service of the Lord, the resulting joy is greater than any you have experienced in other pursuits.

Spend some time meditating on 2 Peter 1:2-8. Then pray expressing your commitment to diligence in learning to walk worthy of Christ in relating to your husband.

Day Three

Romans 15:4   Meditate on **Romans 15:1-4**.

Romans 15:1-3   Notice that the Apostle Paul is discussing the importance of seeking the good of others rather than just pleasing yourself. That is a difficult assignment. It certainly goes against our nature. In countless ways, the world tells us to look out for #1 – make sure you take care of yourself – be fulfilled by fulfilling your every desire, but the Lord desires us to be characterized by love. In fact, He told us that love for others is what would cause us to be recognizable as Christians.

> *By this all men will know that you are My disciples,*
> *if you have love for one another.*
> *John 13:35*

However, a lifestyle of giving preference to the needs of others will give them the opportunity to take advantage of you. How can you maintain a loving attitude while being unfairly used? The answer is in verse four: *For whatever was written in earlier times was written for our instruction.* God has provided His word, the Bible, to guide us and correct us when our attitudes begin to sour.

Romans 15:4   Giving preference to others sometimes results in a lack of appreciation or being taken advantage of. When that happens, you may be tempted to give up. You have learned in prior chapters that you must place your hope in Christ and in His promises.

Romans 15:4 points out two things that, when applied together, restore hope. What are they?

Day Four

Hebrews 12:1-3   Let's return to meditate on Hebrews 12:1-3 again. The last half of verse three speaks of growing weary and losing heart. These are dangerous enemies of perseverance. God's will is often very difficult. The Bible likens persevering in doing God's will to a long-distance race. There will be times when you are exhausted and discouraged. Hebrews 11 and 12 provide encouragement and counsel for those times.

Read **Hebrews 11:1-40** Contemplate the lives of the people mentioned in Hebrews 11. They chose to persevere even when circumstances were difficult, fearful, or painful. Why?

Hebrews 12:1-3   Meditate on what Jesus endured for you. What did Jesus do to strengthen His resolve to persevere?

_____

Christ is your example in perseverance. What should you do when you are weary or discouraged?

_____

_____

Day Five

John 10:1-30   Perseverance is evidence of the reality of your salvation. Read John 10. Take special note of the relationship of the Shepherd to the sheep. The Shepherd is Jesus. If you are a child of God, you are one of His sheep. Based on the verses below, describe your relationship to Jesus in your own words.

John 10:1-3 _____

John 10:4 _____

John 10:5 _____

John 10:7-9 _____

John 10:10 _____

John 10:14-15 _____

John 10:27 _____

John 10:28 _____

John 10:29-30 _____

The concept of perseverance has two meanings in the Bible. What you have learned about on days 1-4 of this chapter is the commitment to never give up in doing God's will regardless of circumstances. In some Bible passages, "perseverance" is used to describe the truth that a true believer cannot lose their salvation. This fundamental teaching of Christianity is called *The Perseverance of the Saints.* It states that all true believers will be saved. Though trial and suffering come, they will not fall away from the faith. Therefore, all true believers will "persevere" (Hebrews 3:5-6 & 14). Those who fall away were never true believers, and were never saved (1 John 2:19). Knowing for certain that you will endure to the end and receive all that God has promised is an important part of being able to persevere in a moment of trial.

Based on your observations (above) about your relationship to Jesus, do you believe in *The Perseverance of the Saints*? _____

If you are unsure of your salvation, do the Bible study entitled *Salvation Handbook* found in **Appendix B.**

Your Thoughts

_____
_____
_____
_____
_____
_____
_____
_____
_____
_____
_____
_____
_____
_____
_____
_____
_____
_____
_____
_____
_____
_____
_____

Chapter 10
Opening your Heart:
Love God and Your Husband

Hannah's Story

I write this last part of my story with joy in my heart. That was not always so. I have been waiting, not knowing how to end my part of the book. I did not want to discourage you, but to be honest, that is what I felt: discouraged. It has been about seven months since I last wrote; unable to write to you. But I have now come to understand that you *need* to know what I went through, the struggles and pitfalls. When I stopped writing, it was on the one year anniversary of the day I my heart was broken. I became completely overwhelmed and discouraged because it was a year out and I still felt no emotional feelings for David. I was faithfully loving him in my actions ~ making love, caring for him, even enjoying him as a friend, but inside I was still numb – nothing. Even when we made love, I was empty inside. I allowed myself to become bitter once again, but this time it was directed at God: "Why had He not given me feelings when I had worked so hard for so long?" I gave up emotionally. I was outwardly loving David, but inside I was hopeless and frustrated. Then, one day I was given this counsel: "Hannah, maybe God wants you to love David in such a way that Ddavid never knows you feel nothing." I said, "Why?" She said simply, "Think of how much glory it would give God for you to love David, even though you feel nothing, and him not to be able to tell." So, I took that on as my task. I kept telling myself to not let David know I felt nothing. You may be saying, "Well it's too late. I already told my husband that." I had too, which made it harder for me to hide. But I kept going, one day at a time, then one week at a time, reminding myself, "He should never know. It is to give God glory." One day David told me that I had changed. I couldn't see it, but he could. So I kept loving. Months past, and one day I looked at David and my heart said, "I love him!" I was shocked. I was happy! My broken heart was healing. I did not tell David then, but waited weeks. I wanted to make sure it was real. The day I told him it took me hours to work up the nerve. I told him, "I love you," and he was so happy

I share this to encourage you not to give up. Don't love with the hope of feeling or being loved. Love to glorify God. I know it seems impossible, but with God you can. It was almost seventeen months before my heart felt anything but pain. But now I can say it: "My broken heart has been a good gift from God. God has grown both David and me, and we are closer now than ever. So guard your heart against those bitter feelings, and guard your mind against hateful thoughts. Put on love and keep going. God is good. He will sustain you. Allow yourself time to grieve and cry, but don't wallow. Pick yourself up, function, go the extra mile. Love -- it is a choice.

Thank you for walking with me through my journey. The process of putting it down for you has been a tremendous blessing for me. I am praying for you, not by name, but in accord with the pain I knew so well.

Hannah

Getting God's Perspective

In chapter nine you were encouraged to have perseverance. The need for perseverance implies the truth that pleasing results may not be quick in coming. Working with damaged marriages in my counseling ministry has taught me that you can expect progress, while trending upward, to be up and down. At times you will be lifted up by a wave of obvious answered prayer and positive change in your marriage. That wave may be followed by a wave of discouragement as you experience a setback. These ups and downs may recur again and again. In the down times you must guard against losing heart. The key is to remember what you have learned about God.

This I recall to my mind, therefore I have hope.
The Lord's lovingkindnesses indeed never cease, for His compassions never fail.
They are new every morning; great is Thy faithfulness.
Lamentations 3:21-23

And we know that God causes all things to work together for good to those who love God,
To those who are called according to His purpose ...
(that we be) conformed to the image of His Son.
Romans 8:28-29

For I am confident of this very thing,
that He who began a good work in you will perfect it until the day of Christ Jesus.
Philippians 1:6

Day One:

1 John 4:7-12   God's love is unwavering. James 1:17 states that with God there is no variation or shifting shadow. God is love.[4] That is why we _know_ that God causes all things to work together for good.[5] Meditate on **1 John 4:7-12**. What is the greatest manifestation of God's love?

---

[4]   1 John 4:16
[5]   Romans 8:28

1 John 4:11   What is the reasonable response to God's love?

_____

1 John 4:8   The "love" referred to in 1 John 4 is consistent, unmerited, loving action without regard to the emotional response of either the loved one or the lover. It is not an emotion. It is a commitment to action. It is God-like love: God loves you in spite of your sin, even though your sin is a source of revulsion to Him. God hates your sin so much He poured out His wrath on Christ because He bore your sin, and yet, His love for you is lavish and unfailing.

According to 1 John 4:8, what is the inescapable conclusion if you refuse to love others (i.e. your husband)?

_____

1 John 4:7, 12   If you choose to love your husband (and others) in response to God's love for you, what does this indicate about you?

_____

_____

Day Two

1 Peter 1:1-9   *"Though you have not seen Him, you love Him ... obtaining as the outcome of your faith the salvation of your souls."* There are many reasons to love the Lord. Read 1 Peter 1:1-9 and list all the things Peter mentions that God did for you (if you are His child).

_____

_____

_____

_____

_____

_____

_____

_____

_____

_____

Revelation 2:1-7   If your love for the Lord has cooled, Christ has advice for you. The church a Ephesus had been a tremendously fruitful church. In fact, they were still very fruitful ... outwardly. However, they had left their first love. They were working for the Lord, but their passion for Him had cooled. What was the Lord's advice to the Ephesian Christians?

_____

_____

In addition to remembering and doing the things that characterized their life when they were first saved, they were told to "repent." Repentance involves three actions:

1. Recognize that your current attitudes and/or behavior are sinful. In this case, what sin were the Ephesian Christians committing? _____

   _____

2. Turn from your sin. Actually commit to doing whatever is necessary to stop sinning in that way.

3. Make a conscious plan (with practical steps) to do the godly alternative. What definite action plan does the Lord command the Ephesian Christians to implement?

   _____

   _____

In light of the Lord's advice to the Ephesian church, what could you do to cultivate love for the Lord? (Be specific, make a practical plan, and implement.)

_____

_____

_____

_____

Day Three

Colossians 3:12-17   This is another passage that we have studied before, but it is of special relevance in the light of Hannah's narrative. Meditate on it today. Take particular note of the command to "put on love." Each morning, while you are dressing, make putting on love an intentional part of your routine. While you shower, make a prayerful commitment to aggressively loving your husband that day for the Lord's sake. While you are getting ready be thinking of specific ways that you can love your husband that day. When you are ready for the day, write down the ways you plan to show love to him that would fit into your day's activities. Begin putting your plan into action.

Hannah elevated her loving actions above the goal of restoring love within her marriage. She focused on loving God so exclusively that even loving David was actually an act of worship. To accomplish this she intentionally went into stealth mode, adding to what she was already doing by loving David in ways that he would not likely notice. This is one of my favorite homework assignments that I give to women I counsel. God uses it in remarkable ways. The net effect is real change in the attitudes and emotions of the women. Try it. You will likely find that it is actually fun! For starters, write down ten things that you could do for your husband that he might not notice. One thing I do for my husband is to clean his bathroom sink several times a week and not just on the day I clean the bathroom.

1. _____
2. _____
3. _____
4. _____
5. _____
6. _____
7. _____
8. _____
9. _____
10. _____

Day Four

Titus 2:3-5   One final reminder: Show tender affection to your husband. There are three distinct words for love in the ancient language in which Titus was written. The word used in Titus 2:3-5 is tender affectionate love. This requires more than just meeting his needs or even giving preference to his desires. I don't need to explain it. You know what tender affection is. For example, write down five things that you would interpret as expressing tender affection if they were done for you.

1. _____
2. _____
3. _____
4. _____
5. _____

Now, from now on, till death do you part, make that kind of behavior a prominent quality of your love for your husband. It is one of the most powerful things you can do to please God.

Now, write down five things that *your husband* would interpret as expressions of tender affection. Remember that what you interpret as tender affection may not be what your husband would interpret as tender affection.

1. _____

2. _____

3. _____

4. _____

5. _____

Day Five

For 50 days I have pointed you to God's word for guidance, encouragement, and comfort. I have every confidence that you have been blessed. The blessing did not come from anything Naomi and I have written. The blessing came from interacting with God's word every day. Today, like a mama bird, I kick you out of the nest with confidence you can fly. But flying will require that you continue to come to God's word every day.

How blessed is the (woman) who does not walk in the counsel of the wicked...
But (her) delight is in the law of the LORD,
And in His law (she) meditates day and night.
And (she) will be like a tree firmly planted by streams of water,
Which yields its fruit in its season,
And its leaf does not whither;
And in whatever (she) does, (she) prospers.
Psalm 1:1-3

Today's your assignment is to begin a daily habit of feeding on God's word on your own. What follows is some practical suggestions that will help. They are not biblical commands, just advice based on my own experience.

1. Purchase a *Week-At-A-Glance* type of daily journal. In the winter, they sell journals that begin on January 1st. In the summer, they sell the "academic" version that begins on July 1st. (This one is marketed for students and teachers.) When the *Week-At-A-Glance* type of journal is open, the facing pages are divided into six blocks, one block for each work day, and one block for the weekend. You will use the daily blocks to make journal entries recording your daily Bible reading and prayer. The advantage of using this type of calendar-journal is that if you skip a day in your Bible reading, the block will forever be empty, staring at you, reminding you that you didn't keep your commitment to read *every day*. You won't want to see those empty blocks testifying to your failure. This provides a little extra motivation to be consistent. It also is a methodical way to evaluate your progress in being faithful. Get the biggest *Week-At-A-Glance* you can find. If you search, you can find one that has full-sized 8 ½ X 11 pages.

2. Do your Bible reading and prayer at the same time every day. Pick a time and stick to it. This will greatly improve your chances of being consistent.

Most people find that the first thing in the morning is a great time for this. If I leave the house before I do my Bible reading and prayer, I rarely get back to it that day.

3. Follow a structured routine. Here is my suggestion.
   a. Pray briefly for the Lord to give you insight as you read and meditate on His word.

   b. Read a section of the Bible. It should be a complete section. If you are reading from one of the narrative books (the gospels, Acts, the Old Testament historical books, etc.), read an entire story. If you are reading a Psalm, read the *entire* psalm. If you are reading from one of the New Testament epistles, read *at least* an entire paragraph.

   c. "SMAC" the passage you have read. Each letter in the word "SMAC" represents one step in meditation on Scripture. In your daily journal block, write down the answers to the four questions represented by "SMAC."

      S = What does it **S**ay?

      M = What does it **M**ean?

      A = How does it **A**pply to me?

      C = What do I need to **C**onfess and/or **C**hange

   d. Spend time in prayer. Include responsive prayer regarding what you learned as you SMACed the reading for the day. Also pray for yourself, for your husband, for others, and pray about anything you told someone you would pray about. If your church has a prayer request list, work through the list a little each day. Record special requests you pray about in that day's journal block. This allows you to occasionally look back and pray again about these things or observe that God has answered your prayers.

The grace of the Lord Jesus Christ be with you,
Mary

Epilogue by Hannah

I want to leave you with a few more thoughts as you finish this book. During the years since I discovered the reason for my own broken heart, I have been growing, and I have been learning as well. As time goes by, I see more ways that I still need to grow. Mostly I see the need to continually watch out for those seeds of bitterness that we talked about in the book. There are days when I am tempted to allow my thoughts to follow the path of bitterness and dwell on the past or the 'what ifs' of the future. I have to admit that I have failed on some of those days. I then had to fight through that bitterness again, confess yet again to my husband and begin working again. I would encourage you in the weeks, months and years ahead to guard against those pitfalls. When you are in the midst of a disagreement, don't pull out past history. Don't allow your thoughts to go down that path. If you do, you will be sinning. When you choose to not go down that path, you are choosing to love the Lord. That is the goal, to love the Lord by loving your husband. Remember it is a day by day and moment by moment choice.

The second thing I have been learning recently is that no matter how healed you feel or act, your marriage will not be completely healed and your relationship restored, until you truly learn to respect your husband again. Now, if you asked me, I would answer that I was respectful and submissive most of the time. If I truly evaluate my heart, I can see that I need to work on that. I came to realize that it is an area that I held back from David. I did it to punish him, but only ended up causing distance and hurt when I could have been benefiting from appreciating David's great effort to change. I would encourage you to not make this mistake. Remember that you are respecting the position given to your husband by God. You are called to respect your husband. (Eph. 5:33b, *"and the wife must see to it that she respects her husband."*) A wife is called to obey this command even if her husband's behavior is sometimes not respectable.

> *It's respect that's given because it's the Lord who requires that respect be given. Giving loving respect to your husband is God's will -- even when he doesn't deserve it. Watch your actions, and listen to your words. God sees and hears.*[6]

Guard your heart against further damage, by simply obeying the Biblical principles we have shared with you. You and your husband will be blessed, and the Lord will be honored.

Lastly, I would remind you again to seek an older woman to help keep you accountable and until you are able to see the hurt as a good gift from the Lord, <u>don't talk ab</u>out it. Even when you are able to see it as such, sharing should be

[6]   *Disciplines of a Godly Woman* by Barbara Hughes, Crossway Books, Wheaton, Illinois, p. 154.

with the intent of helping another and showing them God's goodness and hope in Him during a time when it seems so hard to see good or to hope.

Knowing He does good for His children, and will perfect us until the day He returns, we have hope.

May the God of all comfort, who comforts us in all our affliction, be with you.

Hannah

Appendices

Appendix A

Psalm 139 Memory Cards

Psalm 139:1-3 O Lord, You have searched me and known me. You know when I sit down and when I rise up; You understand my thought from afar. You scrutinize my path and my lying down, And are intimately acquainted with all my ways.	**Psalm 139:13-14** For You formed my inward parts; You wove me in my mother's womb. I will give thanks to You, for I am fearfully and wonderfully made; Wonderful are Your works, And my soul knows it very well.
Psalm 136:4-6 Even before there is a word on my tongue, Behold, O Lord, You know it all. You have enclosed me behind and before, And laid Your hand upon me. Such knowledge is too wonderful for me; It is too high, I cannot attain to it.	**Psalm 139:15-16** My frame was not hidden from You, When I was made in secret, And skillfully wrought in the depths of the earth; Your eyes have seen my unformed substance; And in Your book were all written The days that were ordained for me, When as yet there was not one of them.
Psalm 139:7-9 Where can I go from Your Spirit? Or where can I flee from Your presence? If I ascend to heaven, you are there; If I make bed in Sheol, behold, You are there. If I take the wings of the dawn, If I dwell in the remotest part of the sea,	**Psalm 139:17-20** How precious also are Your thoughts to me, O God! How vast is the sum of them! If I should count them, they would outnumber the sand. When I awake, I am still with you. O that You would slay the wicked, O God; Depart from me, therefore, men of bloodshed. For they speak against you wickedly, And your enemies take Your name in vain.
Psalm 139:10-12 Even there Your hand will lead me, And Your right hand will lay hold of me. If I say, "Surely the darkness will overwhelm me, And the light around me will be night," Even the darkness is not dark to You, And the night is as bright as the day. Darkness and light are alike to You.	**Psalm 139:21-24** Do I not hate those who hate You, O Lord? And do I not loathe those who rise up against You? I hate them with the upmost hatred; They have become my enemies. Search me, O God, and know my heart; Try me and know my anxious thoughts; And see if there be any hurtful way in me, And lead me in the everlasting way.

Appendix B
How to Become a Child of God

The following Bible study is a reprint of *Salvation Handbook* a copyrighted booklet by Martha Peace designed to be used in evangelism and/or biblical counseling. The authors are very grateful to Ms. Peace and Focus Publishing for granting permission to include *Salvation Handbook* as an Appendix to this book.

Salvation Handbook

is available in convenient booklet form through Focus Publishing (www.focuspublishing.com or 1-800-913-6287).

Salvation Handbook
PART ONE: WHO IS JESUS CHRIST?

The Bible tells us much about Jesus and who He is. Many of the claims were made by Jesus Himself and many were made by others about Him. Look up the following references and write down what these claims are. Before you begin your study, say a brief prayer to God and ask Him to show you if these things are true.

1.   What does Jesus call himself?

   a. John 4:25, 26 _____

   b. John 8:28 and John 9:35-38 _____

   c. Matthew 27:42, 43 _____

"Son of God" and "Son of Man" are Old Testament expressions for the Messiah who was predicted to come. The Prophets in the Old Testament knew that this Messiah was God and that He was worthy of worship. See Daniel 7: 13, 14

2.   What does Jesus claim about Himself?

   a. John 5:39_____

   b. John 6:51_____

   c. John 8:12_____

   d. John 8:58_____

e. John 10:30 & 14:7-9 _____

3. The Trinity is three Divine Persons (God the Father, God the Son, and God the Holy Spirit) who are the same in essence and nature yet with distinct personalities. When God the Son, Jesus, lived here on earth for 33 years, He subordinated himself to the will of God the Father. Why? ___ See Philippians 2:5-8.

_____

_____

4. The Apostle Paul says in his letter to Titus that "God is our Savior." Titus 1:3

a. Whom does Paul then say our Savior is? Titus 1:3, 4

_____

b. What else does Paul say about Jesus? Colossians 1:15, 16

_____

5. Whom did Peter say that Jesus was?

a. Mark 8:27-29 _____

b. 2 Peter 1:1 _____

6. Whom did John the Baptist say that Jesus was?
John 1:29 and 34 _____

7. Whom did the Apostle John say Jesus was?

a. John 1:1, 14 _____

b. Revelation 19:16 _____

8. Whom did God the Father say Jesus was?
Matthew 3:17 _____

9. Who has the authority to forgive sins?

a. Luke 5:21 _____

b. Who forgave the paralytic's sins?
Luke 5:17-20 _____

c. What did Jesus do to prove that He had authority to forgive sins?
Luke 5:21-24 _____

Summary:

Jesus claimed to be God by saying He

- performed the miracles that He did

- He was resurrected from the dead

The teaching of the Bible that Jesus is God is not something that we can explain by human logic. It is a supernatural truth which we believe because God's Spirit illumines the truth to us. Next week, we will study in detail what Jesus did on the cross.

PART TWO: WHAT JESUS DID ON THE CROSS

Just about everyone in America has heard of Jesus and knows that He died on the cross. However, they may have many misconceptions about the purpose of His death. So, this week's lesson is a study on "What Jesus Did on the Cross."

1. How was Jesus killed? Matthew 27:35

    _____

2. What did the sign over His head say? Mark 15:26

    _____

3. What did the people say who were making fun of Jesus? Luke 23:35-37

    _____

4. How did the soldiers decide to divide up Jesus' garments? John 19:24

    _____

5. Which four books in the Bible contain the story of Jesus' death on the cross?

    _____

6. Make a list of what Jesus said as He was on the cross:

    a. Luke 23:34 _____

    b. Luke 23:42, 43_____

    c. Luke 23:46 _____

    d. John 19:25, 26_____

    e. John 19:30 _____

    f. Mark 15:37, 38 _____

7. What was the <u>purpose</u> of Jesus' death?

   a. 1 Peter 2:24

   _____

   b. Hebrews 2:17 ("propitiation" means to satisfy God's wrath)

   _____

   c. Ephesians 1:7 ("In Him" refers back to Jesus Christ)

   _____

   d. Romans 4:25 ("He" refers back to Jesus)

   _____

   e. Romans 5:9

   _____

   f. I Corinthians 15:3

   _____

Jesus told His disciples that the "Scriptures" (The Old Testament) were about Him. (John 5:39) Indeed, there are many places in the Old Testament that foretell of the coming Messiah and what He will do for the people so that they can be reconciled to God. (Sin had put a barrier between people and God because God is holy.) Jesus' death on the cross was God's way of punishing sin so that God's sense of justice could be satisfied. In other words, Jesus was punished in our place.

One of the most detailed descriptions of how Jesus took our punishment is in Isaiah 53. This was written by Isaiah over 700 years before Jesus was born. God gave this information to Isaiah supernaturally and Isaiah doesn't call Jesus by His name but calls him the "Servant".

8. How was Jesus treated by men? Isaiah 53:3

   _____

9. What did He "bear" for us? Isaiah 53:4

   _____

10. What happened to Jesus because of our "transgressions" (our sins) and our "iniquities" (also means sins)? Isaiah 53:5

    _____

11. Isaiah 53:5 says, "The chastening (punishment that we deserve) for our _____ fell upon Him."

12. Isaiah 53:6 says, "But the LORD has caused the iniquity (sin) of us all to

_____ _____ _____ "

13.   What kind of sacrificial offering was Jesus? Isaiah 53:10

_____

14.   Where was Jesus' anguish? Isaiah 53:11

_____

15.   What will He bear? Isaiah 53:11

_____

16.   Isaiah 53:12, "Yet He Himself bore the _____ "

17.   What was God's motive for sending Jesus to die for our sins? I John 4:10

_____

Summary: Jesus died on the cross to take the punishment for our sins. He died in our place. He paid the full penalty and then He said,

"IT IS FINISHED!"

PART THREE:
WHAT DOES THE BIBLE TEACH ABOUT SIN?

Last week we studied Jesus' death on the cross and we learned that He died to take the punishment for our sin. Also, we learned that God was satisfied that sin had been sufficiently punished and that Jesus' resurrection from the dead is proof of that. Today, we are going to study about sin --- who sinned first, why they did, and why and how we sin today. Some sins are very obvious -- for example, murder. Some sins are obvious only to God. Regardless of which kind of sin we commit, all sin grieves God because He is perfectly pure and holy. Therefore, we need to understand just what sin is and how to properly deal with it.

1.   The first created being to sin was an angel name Lucifer (later his name became Satan). His problem was pride. He wanted to be worshipped like God was worshipped by some of the other angels. Lucifer made a "power-play" in heaven and God cast Lucifer and all his followers out. What did Lucifer want? See Isaiah 14:13-14. List the five "I will" statements of Lucifer:

   a. _____

   b. _____

c. _____

d. _____

e. _____

2. Lucifer had a real problem with pride. He should have been grateful to worship and serve God. Instead, he wanted all the attention himself. What was the underlying reason that he thought he deserved that kind of attention? Ezekiel 28:17

_____
_____

3. Lucifer was the first angel to sin and Adam and Eve were the first human beings to sin. When God created Adam and Eve they were innocent and without sin. God put them in the Garden of Eden which had a perfect environment and then God tested their devotion to Him and God told them they could eat fruit off any tree except one—"the tree of the knowledge of good and evil." God warned them that if they disobeyed, they would die.

a. Satan was not content to leave well enough alone. He decided to try to get Adam and Eve to follow him by disobeying God. He appeared to Eve in the form of a serpent. See Genesis 3:1

1) How is the serpent described?

_____

2) What did he ask Eve?

_____

b. God told Eve if she ate from that tree she would die. What did Satan tell her would happen? Genesis 3:4

_____

c. Whom did Satan tell Eve she would be "like" if she ate? Genesis 3:5

_____

d. What did Eve decide to do? Genesis 3:6

_____

e. Before they sinned, Adam and Eve were very comfortable around God and not afraid of Him. What was their response to God now? Genesis 3:10

_____

f. God confronted them with their sin. Whom did Adam blame? Genesis 3:12

_____

g. Whom did Eve blame? Genesis 3:13

_____

4. Because God is holy, He has to punish sin. He pronounced judgment right then on Satan, Eve, and Adam. What was one part of the punishment? Genesis 3:19

_____

5. After Adam and Eve sinned, they knew sin in a personal, experiential way. It had become part of their natural nature and was then passed down to their children and their children's children, etc. Also, the consequences of sin were passed down.

a. Why did "death spread to all men"? Romans 5:12

_____

b. What is the "just" consequence of sin? Romans 6:23

_____

6. The Bible classifies sin by different terms such as transgression, iniquity, wickedness, evil, disobedience, and unbelief. Look up the following verses and list what the particular sin is:

a. Romans 13:1

_____

b. 1 Corinthians 6:18

_____

c. Ephesians 4:25-29 (these sins are obvious sins)

_____

d. Ephesians 4:31 (these sins may be obvious or may be "mental attitude" sins. Mental attitude sins are sins that we "think" which may or may not result in an additional, obvious sin.)

_____

e. Ephesians 5:18

_____

f. Philippians 4:6

_____

g. James 3:6

_____

h. James 4:17

_____

     i.   James 5:12

_____

7.   All sin, whether open or hidden, is seen and remembered by God. What does God judge? Hebrews 4:12

_____

8.   Is there anything hidden from God? Hebrews 4:13

_____

9.   God is holy. Therefore, He must punish sin. Man sins. Therefore, man is separated from God and the result is death. However, God loves man. So, He provided a way for man's sins to be punished and for man to be with Him for all eternity. The way that God provided is "Jesus death on the cross bearing our punishment." How is it that we can know that we, personally, are in a right relationship with God? That <u>our</u> sins are taken care of? See Acts 16:31

_____

_____

_____

10.   Oftentimes, people know about Jesus but they are still depending partly on themselves to be good enough to earn their way into heaven. If that's the case, then they are not really "believing" (trusting) in Jesus' death on the cross to be sufficient to save them. The Bible says that Jesus saves us "not on the basis of deeds which we have done, but according to His mercy." (Titus 3:5) In addition to not trusting the Lord Jesus as their Savior, many people are like Satan in that they do not want God to rule over them. They want to control their own lives, so they do not trust Christ as their Lord. If that is true of you, "God is now declaring to men that all everywhere should repent, because He has fixed a day in which He will judge the world in righteousness through a Man (Jesus Christ) whom He has appointed, having furnished proof to all men by raising Him from the dead" (Acts 17:30-31). Romans 10:9 tells us "if you confess with your mouth Jesus as Lord, and believe in your heart that God raised Him from the dead, you shall be saved."

PART FOUR: ASSURANCE OF SALVATION

Many times when people are asked the question, "Do you know <u>for sure</u> that if you died you would go to heaven?" their answer is something like, "I'm not sure but I hope so." Today, our lesson will focus on what the Bible teaches about "knowing for sure." Because this issue is a critical one, before you begin to answer the questions, say a short prayer and ask God to show you the truth of His Word.

1.   A person who is "saved" is going to heaven when he dies. What do you have to "do" to get "saved?"

     See John 3:16 _____

     See Romans 10:13 _____

     See John 1:12 _____

2.   Read the following verses and make a chart. On the left side, list what "saves" you and on the right side, list what will <u>not</u> "save" you:

     John 14:6

     Ephesians 2:8, 9

     Acts 16:30, 31

     Ephesians 2:4, 5

     Colossians 1:13, 14

     Galatians 1:3, 4

     Titus 3:4-7

3.   People think about their salvation one of two ways...

     they must be good and do things to "earn" it, or Jesus did <u>all</u> the work necessary and they must put their faith or "trust" in Him (alone) to be their Savior.

     a.   <u>Nowhere does the Bible say that a person is saved by what he does or how good he is!!!</u> On the contrary, the Bible says that the only acceptable sacrifice or punishment for sins is Jesus' sacrifice on the cross. Why, then, do so many people think they must believe in Jesus <u>plus</u> "earn" their way into heaven? Because, it is logical from a human perspective. But God says, "My ways are not your ways and my thoughts are higher than your thoughts." We're not holy so we do not think like God thinks. Because He's holy, <u>all</u> sin must be punished. It is not enough for us to have done more good things than bad. All the bad had to be dealt with and that's what Jesus declared when He said, "It is finished!"

    b. Look up the following verses and write down what God wants you to know about "assurance of your salvation."

       1. Romans 3:28 _____

       2. Romans 8:1 _____

       3. Romans 10:11 _____

       4. John 5:24 _____

       5. John 6:47 _____

       6. 1 Corinthians 3:15 _____

       7. 2 Corinthians 1:9-10 _____

       8. 1 John 5:11-13 _____

       9. 1 Peter 1:3-5 _____

       10. Titus 1:2 _____

4.   There are basically three reasons why people don't have the assurance of their salvation:

    a. They didn't know what the Bible teaches, or...

    b. They have never really <u>put their trust in Jesus as their Lord and Savior.</u> Jesus said, "But you do not believe, because you are not of My sheep. My sheep hear My voice, and I know them, and they follow me; and I give eternal life to them, and they shall <u>never</u> perish and no one can snatch them out of My hand." John 10:26-28

    c. There is no evidence of salvation in their life such as a desire for God, a longing to please God, or obedience to Christ's commandments. "And by this we know that we have come to know Him, if we keep His commandments" (I John 2:3).

Salvation is a work of God not a work of man. So if you are having doubts, ask God to grant you repentance from your sin and faith in His Son.

Appendix C
Scriptures Used

The LORD will help you.
> Psalm 6:6-9
> Psalm 23
> Psalm 32:10
> Psalm 55:1-22
> Isaiah 41:8-14
> Isaiah 43:1-3a
> Philippians 4:4:19
> 2 Peter 1:2-8

The LORD watches over you.
> Psalm 23
> Psalm 33:18
> Psalm 34:15
> Psalm 139

Satisfaction is found in the LORD.
> Psalm 63:1-8

The one who trusts God is blessed.
> Psalm 37:1-8
> Proverbs 3:5-8
> Jeremiah 17:5-10
> 2 Corinthians 3:14-18
> Philippians 4:4-7
> 1 Peter 5:6-10
> 2 Peter 1:19-21
> Revelation 2:1-7

Counsel to wives.
> Proverbs 31:10-31
> Ephesians 5:22-24, 33
> 1 Peter 2:19 – 3:6

Do not fear.
> Isaiah 41:8-14
> Isaiah 43:1-3a

Promises of joy.
> Isaiah 55:12
> Isaiah 66:10-14

Hope.
> Lamentations 3:19-32
> Romans 5:1-11
> 1 Peter 1:1-9

Dealing with sin.
> Matthew 7:3-5
> Matthew 18:15-20
> John 8:1-11
> Galatians 6:1-4

Stumbling blocks.
> Luke 17:1-4

The Gospel.
> John 10:1-30

Wisdom for knowing what to say.
> Proverbs 11:9, 12-13
> Proverbs 18:19

Wisdom regarding anger.
> Proverbs 30:33
> Matthew 5:21-22

Responding to abuse.
> Matthew 5:39, 43-45
> Romans 12:14, 17-21
> 2 Corinthians 4:7-18
> 1 Peter 2:19 – 3:1-6, 8-10

Seek counsel from God's word.
> Romans 15:1-6, 14
> Psalm 1:1-3

Love.
> 1 Corinthians 13:1-13
> Colossians 3:12-17
> 1 Thessalonians 5:11, 14-15
> 1 John 4:7-12

Comfort.
> 2 Corinthians 1:2-5
> Romans 5:1-11
> Galatians 4:1-7

God controls circumstances.
> Romans 8:26-29
> Lamentations 3:19-32

Controlling your thoughts.
> 2 Corinthians 10:3-5

Forgiveness.
> 2 Corinthians 2:4-11
> Ephesians 4:29 – 5:2
> Hebrews 12:14-15

Habit replacement.
> Ephesians 4:17-32

Gossip.
> Proverbs 11:9, 12-13
> 1 Timothy 3:11
>
> 1 Timothy 5:13
> 2 Timothy 3:1-5
> Titus 2:305

Endurance.
> Hebrews 11:30 - 12:8

Appendix D
Resources for Your Mentor
Habit Replacement:
The Put-Off-Put-On Dynamic
Developed by Martha Peace

This Bible study teaches Christians how to deal practically with their sin. Many times we are aware that changes need to be made in our lives and we confess the appropriate sins to God. However, we may find ourselves committing those same sins again and again. Habitual sin is especially difficult because we automatically respond wrongly, without thinking. Therefore, it is important to learn exactly what God teaches us through His Word about establishing new habit patterns.

Before you begin this study, pray and ask God to show you the truth of His Word.

Begin by looking up the following Scriptures and write out the answers to the questions.

1.   How do we become aware of sin?

    a) Hebrews 4:12

    b) John 16:7-8

2.   Do we <u>have</u> to sin? Explain. (See Romans 6:6, 7,14.)

3.   Describe what the "old self" was like. (See Ephesians 4:22.)

4.   Describe what the "new self" is like. (See Ephesians 4:24.)

5.   What are we to "put off" and what are we to "put on"? (See Ephesians 4:22, 24.)

6.   What are we to "put off" (lay aside) according to Colossians 3:9?

7. What are we to "put on" according to Colossians 3:10?

8. This "new self" is to be renewed. How? (See Colossians 3:10.)

Thus, we see that we are to "put off" our old ways of thinking and acting and "put on" new ways which are like those of Jesus Christ. When sinful ways of thinking or responding have become habitual, just confessing that sin is not enough. The sinful habit pattern must be <u>replaced</u> with a righteous habit pattern. It is as if what we are to "put on" is the biblical antidote to what we are to "put off". For example, it is not enough to just stop telling lies. A person must begin (work at) telling the truth, the whole truth. By God's help (grace) he will become a truthful person instead of a liar.

Look up the following Scriptures and fill in the chart:

Scripture Reference	"Put Off" Character Deficiencies	"Put On" Character Qualities
1. Ephesians 4:25		
2. Ephesians 4:26,27		
3. Ephesians 4:28		
4. Ephesians 4:29		
5. Ephesians 4:31,32		
6. Ephesians 5:11		
7. Ephesians 5:4		
8. Ephesians 5:18		

9. Philippians 4:6		
10. Colossians 3:8,12,13,14		
11. Romans 13:12-14		

As we have seen earlier, God gives Christians the Holy Spirit to convict them of sin and to help them carry out God's desires. As a result, is there anything that God requires that a Christian cannot do? (See Philippians 4:13.) Hence, God will never ask us to do something that He will not give us the grace to carry out. Sometimes we may not feel like obeying God; however, if we do obey (in spite of our feeling), God will give us grace.

Write down the specific sins in your life you know need to be "put off".

Take time now to confess these sins to God.

Write down what you are to "put on" (biblical antidote) in your life in the place of these sins:

Write down some practical actions you can do to "put on" godly character:

1. _____

2. _____

3. _____

4. _____

5. _____

6. _____

Based upon what you have learned in this study, write out your prayer:

_____

_____

_____

_____

_____

_____

_____

_____

_____

_____

_____

_____

_____

_____

_____

_____

_____

_____

_____

_____

Recommended Books
and Other Discipleship Resources

1. How to be a godly wife:
    The Excellent Wife by Martha Peace.
    Focus Publishing

2. Knowing God:
    Trusting God Even When Life Hurts by Jerry Bridges.
    Navpress.

    The Attributes of God by A.W. Pink

3. Dealing with adversity and suffering:
    Trusting God Even When Life Hurts by Jerry Bridges.
    Navpress.

4. The fundamentals of Christian living:
    Fundamentals of the Faith by John MacArthur
    Moody Publishers

5. Finding a good church:
    Life in The Father's House by Wayne Mack
    P & R Publishing

6. Knowing God's will:
    Discovering God's Will by Sinclair Ferguson.
    Banner of Truth

    God's Will is Not Lost by John MacArthur. Out of print, but can be
    purchased as a used booklet through Amazon .com

7. Thinking biblically about psychology and psychology based counseling:
    The Christian's Guide to Psychological Terms by Marshall and Mary Asher
    Focus Publishing

    Psychologized Man by Martha Peace
    Focus Publishing

    From Freud to Jesus by Richard Ganz (DVD)
    Stock #N9507DVD, Sound Word, www.soundword.com.
    (219) 548-0933

8. Depression:
    Out of the Blue by Wayne Mack
    Focus Publishing

9. Bitterness
    Bitterness The Root That Pollutes by Lou Priolo
    P&R Publishing

10. How to counsel:
    Ready to Restore by Jay Adams. The Layman's Guide to Christian
    Counseling.
    Presbyterian and Reformed Publishing Company.

    Quick Scripture Reference for Counseling Women by Patricia A. Miller.
    Baker Books.